# EIGHTEEN AMAZING WOMEN PHILOSOPHERS

Originally published by Decoded Science (2014) as
*Fifteen Women Philosophers you should have learned
at school (but probably didn't)*

Revised and republished

By Janet Cameron MA (2019)

The under-representation of women in philosophy is an unfortunate truth. The development of women's philosophical work today spans the three waves of feminism starting in the late 1800s. This history did not spring from a vacuum. Before the early suffragettes lies a plethora of amazing, smart-thinking women prepared to speak up and to suffer for their beliefs.

From brave Hypatia of Alexandria and bookworm Maria le Jars de Gournay, to the stunning Mary Wollstonecraft, who was so far advanced in her thinking that we can only wonder at her great achievement - these women blazed trails for feminism, even though, in their time, the word "feminism" had not been created.

Join award-winning author, retired lecturer Janet Cameron, MA as she explores eighteen female philosophers you may never have heard of - women who changed the world, and the way we think today.

# CONTENTS

INTRODUCTION ~ 5

CHAPTER 1 HYPATIA ~ 8

CHAPTER 2 MURASAKI SHIKIBU ~ 13

CHAPTER 3 MARIE LE JARS DE GOURNAY ~ 19

CHAPTER 4 MARY WOLLSTONECRAFT ~ 24

CHAPTER 5 SOJOURNER TRUTH ~ 29

CHAPTER 6 ERNESTINE ROSE ~ 34

CHAPTER 7 ADA LOVELACE ~ 39

CHAPTER 8 ELIZABETH CADY STANTON ~ 45

CHAPTER 9 AYN RAND ~ 50

CHAPTER 10 HANNAH ARENDT ~ 56

CHAPTER 11 SIMONE DE BEAUVOIR ~ 62

CHAPTER 12 SIMONE WEIL ~ 67

CHAPTER 13 PHILIPPA FOOT ~ 74

CHAPTER 14 ELIZABETH ANSCOMBE ~ 81

CHAPTER 15 IRIS MURDOCH ~ 87

CHAPTER 16 MARY WARNOCK ~ 94

CHAPTER 17 MARY MIDGLEY ~ 99

CHAPTER 18 MARY BEARD ~ 111

Conclusion ~ 116

Bibliography ~ 117

About the Author ~ 123

# Introduction

Why a book on women philosophers? After all, a great philosopher is just that – a great philosopher. The post is genderless, like a great poet or a great composer.

However, the under-representation of women in philosophy is an unfortunate truth. In her article: *Name Five Women in Philosophy, Bet You Can't* in *Cosmo and Culture*, July 17, 2013, Tania Lombrozo met with academics researching this worrying discrepancy, to learn about their findings.

The article concludes that the philosopher, Hegel, was wrong when he said that women's minds were not adapted to the higher sciences.

The researchers, says Lombrozo, have found that the problem is compounded by bias. She quotes Morgan Thompson of Georgia State University:

*"This problem is compounded by the fact that introductory philosophy textbooks have an even worse gender balance; women account for only 6 percent of authors in a number of introductory philosophy textbooks."*

The development of women's philosophical work today spans the three waves of feminism starting from the late 1800s. However, this history did not spring from a vacuum. Before the early suffragettes, lies a plethora of amazing, smart-thinking women prepared to speak up and to suffer for their beliefs, for example, brave Hypatia of Alexandria, bookworm Maria le Jars de Tournay, and the stunning Mary Wollstonecraft, who was so far advanced in her thinking that we can only wonder at her great achievement.

At this time, the word "feminism" had not been created.

The first wave of feminism has its roots around the time of the Seneca Falls Convention in 1848, attended by 300 men and women. A declaration of an ideology and political strategy was established with the intention to open up opportunities for women. Out of this came female suffrage.

It was a time of industrialisation and liberal social politics. The women's movement was closely inter-related with the abolitionist movement. Unlike the later waves of feminism, most of the women activists were white and middle-class. Their "unladylike behaviour" of public speech and demonstration landed many of them in jail.

The second wave of feminism began during the 1960s, ran through to around the early 1990s, and became part of a larger combination of issues, for example, the anti-war campaign, civil rights and the concerns of many minority groups.

There were protests against the Miss America pageant in Atlantic City in 1968 and 1969, and feminists made fun of the "cattle parade" that they claimed reduced women to sexual objects. A sheep was crowned "Miss America" and women burned their bras and discarded feminine fripperies.

Women refused to be subjugated by a patriarchal society. They wanted freedom, education and financial and sexual independence.

Some said that sexuality was biological, but gender was a social construct.

The third wave of feminism occurred during the mid-1990s, when women became empowered and chose to retain their feminine beauty for themselves. They re-claimed such slurs as "slut" and "bitch" in order to subvert the sexist culture. Thus we had the "cybergrrrls" and the "netgrrrls." It became possible to cross gender boundaries. This trend became global and multicultural.

*Unladylike Behaviour!  Photo by Gareth Cameron*

From the necessary feminist philosophy of the first and second wave movements, came a trend towards an applied philosophy, at which women excel. Women asked how we could use philosophy to teach us how to live better?  As a result, we have many great female moral and ethical philosophers today. Great women philosophers, for example, the late Iris Murdoch, even brought metaphysics to theories of morality.

Women, just like men, want to identify with and relate to the subjects that interest them. I hope this book will go some way to address this under-representation of women in the academic world, but even more importantly, in our everyday thinking.

# Chapter 1

# Hypatia of Alexandria: Philosopher and the First Notable Woman Mathematician

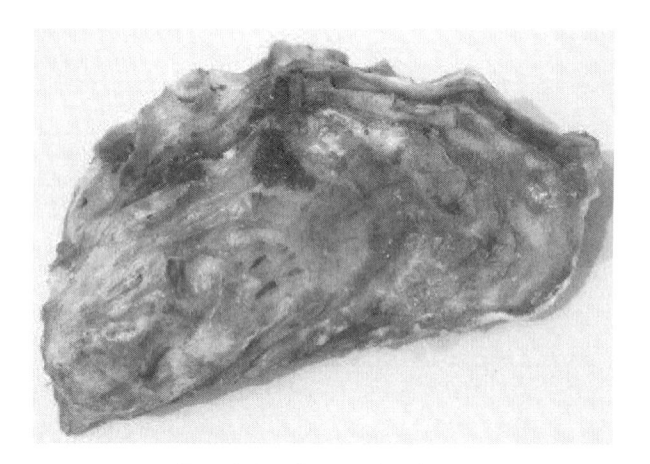

Death by Oyster Shells –
Believed to be Hypatia's fate for her eminence among men.
Image by David Monniaux.

Why is Hypatia, who lived in Alexandria, a rarity merely for being a female philosopher in the ancient world? In fact, why have there been so few female philosophers throughout history – just a few in Egypt – at least until the birth of feminism when women began to find their voices?

When we learn what happened to this fabulous woman, it's not surprising few cared to follow in her footsteps.

We have no written evidence from Hypatia herself, so it can be difficult pinning down what is true. Other anecdotes about her can be found in the bibliography at the end of this book.

## *Diving into the Wreck* of Women's Lost Past

Hypatia was an early victim to the myth that women cannot, or are not entitled, to achieve excellence and receive accolades in academic study. It is claimed she was extremely beautiful and shapely, and, unfortunately this did not help her cause.

In her poem, *Diving into the Wreck*, the American poet, Adrienne Rich, presents a challenge to women everywhere to recover the evidence of the brilliance of their lost "grandmothers." For there are many great women like Hypatia whose stories still lie buried.

The title *Diving into the Wreck* is, in fact, a metaphor for the long and painstaking project to find the hidden evidence of women of the past and to recognise the price they paid for their resistance to the negative conditions of their environment. The truth is that we stand on their shoulders.

Essentially, Rich is struggling to find her way to reality, by blazing a trail through the myths of the past. We must achieve understanding, and in its wake, redemption. With Rich, we struggle to engage and become involved with our past and to discover the truth behind the names we barely know and to which we owe so much.

## Hypatia's Background

Despite the terrible trials for the women of the past, Hypatia's life story is especially chilling, even though accolades preserved from her time are full of admiration for her dignity and virtue.

Hypatia was the daughter of the philosopher, Theon Alexandricus, (335-405 AD) and she was fortunate in that her father nurtured her intelligence and encouraged her to feel confident amongst her peers. He treated her exactly as other good fathers would treat their sons.

Theon's progressive ways led to Hypatia attaining knowledge in science, logic and astrology; we remember her as the first notable female mathematician. She and her father followed in the footsteps of the great philosophers, Plato and Plotinus.

The following quotation from the *Ancient and Classical History* website explains one of her great gifts to mathematics: *"By writing a commentary on The Conics of Apollonius of Perga, which divided cones into sections by a plane, Hypatia made geometry intelligible to her students and ultimately transmissible to the modern world."*

Hypatia, philosopher and challenger of assumptions,
died a terrible death at the hands of Peter the Reader
and his cohorts. Drawing by Jules Maurice Gaspard.

## The Insidious Effects of Professional Jealousy

People came from near and far to engage with her philosophical teachings. As a result of her self-possession, she was often required to appear before the magistrates and consort with men of importance. Inevitably, the excellence of her mind led to political jealousy among some of the men, who circulated defamatory stories about her. These stories led to a terrible conclusion.

A nasty piece of work called Peter the Reader led the group of 'Christians' ultimately responsible for Hypatia's fate. Orestes, a governor, had quarrelled with the bishop, St. Cyril of Alexandria, who was, allegedly, a patriarch afflicted with a strong and bigoted temperament. This disagreement had become the cause of great disharmony.

Peter the Reader and his cohorts erroneously reported that Hypatia was intentionally preventing the two men from becoming reconciled.

They had secured a crime and they were going to act upon it.

## Hypatia is Savagely Massacred

Peter and his co-conspirators ambushed Hypatia as she was walking home to her husband, Isidorus. They dragged her out of her chariot, and into a church, known as the Caesarium. Here, within this holy place, they committed an outrage so terrible it is almost beyond comprehension.

They stripped Hypatia of all her garments, and tore into her with sharp oyster shells, scraping away strips of her flesh. Then, they bore her limbs to another place, known as the Cinaron, and there they burnt them.

Realising they had perpetrated a most savage massacre, the killers offered gifts to the authorities to avoid any punishment.

*(According to Socrates Scholasticus, the Greek word for oyster shells, which is "ostrakois" can also mean brick tiles as applied to house roofs.  Oysters shells, however, seem a more efficient and, therefore, more likely method.)*

## Honouring the Spirits of Women from the Past

When Adrienne Rich wrote her poem, *Diving into the Wreck*, she was speaking to women of Hypatia's ilk. Rich, as the poem's narrator, "is looking for "…a book of myths / in which / our names do not appear."

Our grandmothers may have suffered, but we can honour their spiritual truth by discovering, by remembering and by naming them.

# CHAPTER 2

# Murasaki Shikibu – Japanese Feminist and the World's First Novelist

Japanese women today revere Shikubu,
the world's first woman novelist and
feminist philosopher. Image by Imagoo

Murasaki Shikibu (978-1014 AD) is the pen-name of a woman who wrote the world's first novel, a major work of depth and meaning.

This psychological novel was *The Tale of Genji,* the story of a prince who was not sufficiently royal to ascend the throne.

## The Four Female Virtues

Murasaki Shikibu was born in Kyoto. She was educated in Confucian classics which upheld the female virtues of morality, proper speech, a modest appearance, and diligent work.

She was probably a member of the noble Fujiwarer family, which maintained its position through marrying off its daughters to members of the royal family.

Shikibu married around 998 and gave birth to a daughter, but when her husband died around 1001, she entered court and became an attendant to the Empress Akibu. It was there she produced her first and finest work, *The Tale of Genji,* and it was likely the Empress saw Murasaki's work in progress.

The novel was written in Japanese kana language, which is phonetic. Most Japanese men at that time studied in Chinese, but only a few women were fortunate enough to be educated to that level.

Murasaki Shikibu wrote *The Tale of Genji* between 1000 and 1008 AD. There are two other works of note, *The Diary of Lady Murasaki* and *Diaries of Court Ladies of Old Japan.* She was, in addition, an accomplished poet. The time in which she lived is known as the Heian period.

## The Writing Genius of Murasaki Shikibu

This is an exceptional novel, containing all the required attributes of a sophisticated literary work: great content, complexity of plot, deep characterisation, meaningful outcomes and a resolution that is both satisfying and philosophical.

*"The Tale of Marasaki Shikibu"* in *The Economist,* explains that Prince Genji possessed everything (apart from sufficient royal blood) including *"…brains, looks, charm, artistic talent and the love of well-born ladies."*

Genji reinvents himself as a powerful commoner and resorts to womanising at court, by working his way through illicit love affairs and scandalous intrigues. The women he consorts with never attain true happiness, but then, his seduction of the ladies is no more than political opportunism.

Murasaki Shikibu uses sophisticated writing techniques including irony, a technique Victorian novelist Jane Austen exploited some time later to great effect.

In an interview with *The Economist, Haruo Shirane,* professor of Japanese literature at Columbia University in New York, says,

*"The psychology of the characters is complex; the central drama is their eternal conflict."*

Some literary experts compare Shikibu's novel with Proust's *Remembrance of Things Past.* Like Proust's work, *The Tale of Genji* explores memory and passing time.

## The Woman Behind the Pseudonym

We only have fragments to inform us about Murasaki Shikibu and her life and, as mentioned above, we are not even sure of the real name of the world's first novelist. The first name we now use for the woman who wrote *The Tale of Genji, "Murasaki"* means a purple wisteria flower. Her second name, *"Shikibu"* describes her father's position at court in the Bureau of Ceremony.

In one of her diaries, says *The Economist*, she speaks of herself as *"pretty but shy, fond of old tales."*

Murasaki means purple wisteria flower.
Image by marymary00767

## The Inner World of Home

Shikibu's writing seems even more extraordinary when we consider her background. Even as a high-born woman, she was still, in the end, merely a woman in times dominated by men.

Heian women lived in separate compounds from the men and could only talk to them through special screens known as kitcho screens. Unlike women in China, Heian women were allowed to own and inherit property, but their world was an inner world from which they rarely escaped, except perhaps to visit a court festival or take a pilgrimage to a Buddhist temple.

Amanda Foreman, writer and presenter of the BBC2 serial *The Ascent of Women*, explains in Episode 2, *"Separation,"* that Murasaki was responsible for the beginning of literature in Japan. She says the

*"…first flowering of Japanese literature was dominated by women, the most important of whom, in my opinion, was Murasaki Shikibu."*

*The Economist* says,

*"The modern novel was born at the Imperial Court of Japan."*

## Literary Fiction at Court

How did Shikibu produce such a mature work? In *The Tale of Genji*, Shikibu draws on her own knowledge of court life. She emphasises the fragility of love, asking why there is suffering in the world. Shikibu allows her protagonist to discover and find solace in Buddhism which says that all life is suffering, just as Murasaki, in her personal isolation as a Japanese woman, discovers in her own life. She, too, resorts to Buddhism to reconcile the nature of suffering.

Amanda Foreman, in *Separation,* credits Japanese women, especially Murasaki Shikibu, with forging the cultural DNA of her country, a feat seldom achieved by women stuck in subordinate roles to those of men. There is an emotional scene in the programme when Foreman is shown an ancient inkwell, a fragile and delicate artefact, which was probably the one used by Murasaki Shikibu to write her princely tale one thousand years ago. There is a catch in Foreman's voice as she shares with the viewer how profoundly she is affected by this moment and its vital importance to women's history.

## The Legacy of Murasaki Shikibu

Besides being a much-revered role model for modern Japanese women, Murasaki Shikibu's work has engendered a multitude of translations in a number of languages, films and CDs. A British scholar, Arthur Waley, published a version of *The Tale of Genji* through 1925 to 1933.

*"It was his limpid prose,"* says *The Economist, "that brought Genji to western readers as they re-examined Japanese culture after the second [W]orld [W]ar."*

Worldwide admiration for Murasaki Shikibu and her work is hardly surprising. Here is a small snippet from one of her diaries (In *Diaries of Court Ladies of Old Japan*):

*"It is useless to talk with those who do not understand one and troublesome to talk with those who criticize from a feeling of superiority. Especially one-sided persons are troublesome. Few are accomplished in many arts and most cling narrowly to their own opinion."*

— Murasaki Shikibu, *Diaries of Court Ladies of Old Japan.*

Good advice – then and now!

# Chapter 3

# Marie le Jars de Gournay: Early Feminist Who Loved to Read

Noble lady of the 16th century.

Marie le Jars de Gournay (1565-1645) is sometimes known as La Dame de Gournay. She was the first of six children born into a noble family in Paris, but sadly, her father died when she was young and her mother moved the family to Gournay.

She was a unique young woman, for while it would be more natural for a noblewoman like her, according to the culture of her time, to sew, or plan a trousseau; she was more interested in studying, and would slip away at every opportunity to resume her reading.

On the website *Arlea*, Séverine Auffret discusses the young philosopher's unwavering commitment to her passions by saying,

"*Elle préfère lire, se passionner pour les sciences, les lettres et la philosophie.*" (She prefers to read; her passion is for science, literature and philosophy.)

Through her passion, she discovered the essays of the philosopher Michel de Montaigne, and she wrote to him, an act of considerable precociousness at that time. Michel de Montaigne called upon her the following day, and as a result, the two became great friends. He called her his *"adopted daughter."*

## A Philosopher in Her Own Right

Séverine Auffret is anxious to discourage any notion that Marie le Jars de Gournay was a mere *"satellite of a planet,"* in her role as translator and friend to Michel de Montaigne. On the contrary, she was not a mere recipient of his largesse, although, undoubtedly, he was her mentor. Auffret emphasises she was an independent thinker: *"Elle ne fut pas l'humble servant de l'oevre d'un maitre."* (She was not the humble beneficiary of the work of a master.)

She worked hard to translate and promote the work of her admired mentor, but it is essential to recognise that her own work did not depend upon his theories. It's claimed her philosophy is less sceptical than Montaigne's. Among her best-known works are *Equality Between Men and Women,* a subject close to her heart; *Complaints of Ladies*; and *Apology for the Writing Women.* In the latter title, the word *"apology"* doesn't mean an expression of regret for a wrong, but *"the reasons for…."*

She did not spare herself, but learned Latin through the laborious process of comparing the texts and their translations.

## Gournay Addresses Queen Anne of Austria

Séverine Auffret describes how the young Marie had the temerity to write to Queen Anne of Austria, presenting her book, *Equality Between Men and Women.*

Auffret points out that Gournay's style indicates a life that draws broadly from years of obstinate desire to force the hand of her own destiny. John J. Conley, in his article *"Marie le Jars de Gournay,"* says

*"Gournay's extensive literary corpus touches a wide variety of philosophical issues."*

Later, she would become well-known for her own pro-feminist essays.

## Views on Vice and Virtue

According to Gournay, personal honour is the first and most important virtue, while calumny is the greatest vice. She roundly attacks political and religious organisations, addresses their defects and is especially critical of the evils of slander. She mentions, in particular, the spiteful behaviour of courtiers.

However, she has no illusions about the nature of virtue, indicated in this rather convoluted statement.

In a work entitled *Vicious Virtue*, she argues,

*"One cannot remove from humanity all the virtuous actions it practices because of coercion, self-interest, chance, or accident. Even graver are the external virtues which follow on some vicious inclination…To eliminate all such virtuous acts would place the human race closer to the rank of simple animals than I would dare to say."*

It seems she was very much a realist, and wasn't fooled by external appearances.

## Gournay's Attack on Gender Inequality

Inequality of the sexes figures largely in her philosophy, says Auffret, with its *"…malicious prejudice which has barred women from educational and work opportunities."* The inequality between men and women, she blames on the politics of the time, and she says it is based on prejudice. It is a misogyny that reduces women to a state of servitude.

Auffret speaks at length of *"a beautiful series of [Gournay's] works now rediscovered*

*, after being unjustly forgotten: poems, Latin translations, essays, pamphlets – in addition to the valuable editing work that is known."* (Author's translation with a little help from Google Translate.)

## The Metaphysics of Poetry

One of the theories closest to Gournay's heart is her belief in the free rein of neologisms (newly-coined words/phrases not yet accepted into common use) and of metaphor in poetic speech. For her, this freedom to experiment with language has far-reaching metaphysical consequences. She feels that every artisan must be free to work according to his/her own judgment and s/he is entitled to shape it and enrich it, in order to add richness and beauty.

John J. Conley says: *"Not only does metaphor please the senses of the reader; it communicates certain truths about God, nature, and the human soul which cannot be expressed through more concise, abstract rhetoric. Defense of Poetry provides her most extensive analysis of innovation and simile in the poetic expression of truth."*

## Superseded, Forgotten — Then Rediscovered

During her lifetime, Gournay endured many peaks and troughs. When her mother died in 1592, and she arranged the disposal of the family estate, she was overgenerous with her siblings, and, as a result, lived in reduced circumstances for some time. The following year, Montaigne died and his widow asked her to complete a new edition of his essays. She agreed and stayed with Madame de Montaigne for about fifteen months, then went to Holland.

In Paris, she used what influence she had to obtain a pension from Queen Marguerite of Valois, and was also presented at Henry's IV's court. After the King was assassinated in 1610, she faced charges and opposition. After this, says John J. Conley, she was

*"…fair game for ridicule, attack and practical jokes. Even Richelieu poked fun at her."*

Fortunately, her graciousness and good manners helped her to endure, and although she would never fit in, she savoured her intellectual passions and her independence.

By the latter part of the seventeenth century, Michel de Montaigne's material had superseded Gournay's and she fell into obscurity. Fortunately towards the end of the twentieth century, feminists looking for long-forgotten female authors revived her work with the intent on returning to modern women the vital elements of their lost past.

# Chapter 4

# Mary Wollstonecraft:

# The First Feminist Scandalises Society

"It is justice, not charity, that is wanting in the world."
Mary Wollstonecraft. Image by Advocathee1

Mary Wollstonecraft (1759-1797) was born in Spitalfields in London. Her father lost his money farming, and young Mary's life was to undergo a change; she had to become self-sufficient. She received a limited education, but was mostly self-taught, and made her living writing, translating, reading, reviewing and editing.

## A Hyena in Petticoats

Mary scandalised the Church, the Monarchy and her contemporaries for her strident resistance to the established social order. Her revolutionary views made her unpopular to the extent that she was described as "*a hyena in petticoats*" by one male critic, according to Jeremy Harwood, in *100 Great Thinkers.* Mary's primary goal was that women should have access to a proper education and that society should recognise women as equal to men.

She shocked society even more with her uncompromising views in her manifesto, *A Vindication of the Rights of Women,"* declaring,

*"Let women share the rights and she will emulate the virtues of man."*

(A brave and outrageous claim for these difficult times.)

## Male Views of Women in 1700s

Mary Wollstonecraft was incensed, not only by the patriarchal society, but also by women who both tolerated and supported it. These women allowed the world to regard them as beautiful, but did not object if men did not treat them as reasoning human beings.

What was necessary, according to Mary Wollstonecraft, was equality in life.

Wollstonecraft made some allowances for these women, in acknowledging that it was impossible to expect women to be virtuous until they had some degree of equality with men. Their situation in life, which was that of uneducated chattels, reduced them to the level of slaves, and was bound to make them… *"cunning, mean and selfish,"* she wrote in her manifesto.

## Wollstonecraft's Views of Men

Mary is equally scathing towards men: *"Men neglect the duties incumbent of men, yet are treated like demigods."*

At the end of the final chapter of the *Vindication,* she has added some notes, including the following:

*"I once lived in the neighbourhood of one of these men, a handsome man, and saw with surprise and indignation women, whose appearance and attendance bespoke that rank in which females are supposed to reach superior education, flock to his door."*

## Women's Disregard of Order

In *Romantic Writings,* Susan Matthews says,

*"Femininity, according to Wollstonecraft, is characterized by certain mental habits, of which she singles out a female "disregard of order" caused by lack of education."*

Wollstonecraft says Matthews, believes women generalise too much and *"rely too much on sheer observations of real life."*

Matthews asserts that not all women writers in Victorian times wanted to be novelists, as such works were regarded as of low status prior to 1800. However, a successful female novelist needed to hone her powers of observation.

Wollstonecraft remained dismissive of such skills.  Conversely, her contemporary, Jane Austen, believed the observation of real life was the greatest strength of her genre and exploited it to the highest degree.

Plaque for Mary Wollstonecraft, outside
The Polygon, St. Pancras, London,
where she died in 1797. Image by Ellaroth

## A Few Male Spirits in Female Frames

In her book *Of Woman Born*, the great American poet, Adrienne Rich, cites the pain with which Wollstonecraft viewed the *"passive obedience"* and physical weakness she observed in most women she came into contact with. Wollstonecraft imagined that the few extraordinary women she actually met, who *"rushed in eccentrical directions out of the orbit prescribed to their sex,"* were actually male spirits in female frames.

Rich is critical of this stance, just as great novelist, Jane Austen, might have been about Wollstonecraft's attitudes regarding the unimportance of observations. Rich says that fear and hatred affects the brains of brilliant women, who

*"…are still trying to think from somewhere outside their female bodies – hence they are still merely reproducing old forms of intellection."* (sic)

Wollstonecraft also said,

*"Women should think as well as feel if they are to break out of their ideological corsets."*

It's hard not to admire such a fine metaphor, and also easy understand the fury of this exceptional woman. At the same time, we can see why, in such an uncompromisingly patriarchal society, she became an object of disapproval and verbal abuse

## Education for Children

In the *Vindication*, Wollstonecraft insists that there must be more equality in society and that Government should establish day schools, for the education of both boys and girls. From ages five to nine, she says, education should be free.

## The Great Irony of Wollstonecraft's Life

Wollstonecraft's life was tragically cut short, as she died while giving birth to another great writer of a different persuasion – Mary Shelley who wrote the novel, *Frankenstein.* The father of the child was the philosopher and novelist, William Godwin. However, it was not a difficult birth that killed Mary Wollstonecraft, but the general neglect of women in lying-in clinics between the 17th and 19th centuries.

Adrienne Rich in *Of Woman Born,* explains:

*"Meanwhile, the potential sources of the disease went unexplored, and women continued to die – not from giving birth but from acute streptococcal infection of the uterus, in no way linked with the birth-process."*

This must be the greatest and most tragic irony of Mary Wollstonecraft's brief life. What more might this strong woman have achieved for women and the education of minors, if she had not died, so pitifully, at just 38 years old?

# CHAPTER 5

# Sojourner Truth, Abolitionist, Reformer, Champion of Black Women

Sojourner Truth, Carte de Visite
Unknown Photographer.
Image courtesy of Library of Congress

Sojourner Truth was born into slavery, circa 1797, as Isabella Baumfree. She was one of twelve children born to James and Elizabeth Baumfree from Ghana and Guinea, respectively. Colonel Hardenbergh owned the Baumtree family and they lived on his estate in Esopus, New York.

After the colonel's death, his son Charles owned the family, but when Charles himself died in 1806, they were split up, and Sojourner Truth was sold.

## One Slave Girl and a Flock of Sheep: $100

The *Sojourner Truth Biography*, on *A&E TV Networks*, says:

*"The 9-year-old Truth, known as 'Belle' at the time, was sold at an auction with a flock of sheep for $100. Her new owner was a man named John Neely, whom Truth remembered as harsh and violent."*

Slaveholders sold the young slave twice more over the following two years. Previously, 'Bella' spoke only Dutch, but by the time she was living on the property of John Dumont of West Park, New York, she was learning to speak English.

## Sojourner Truth: Escape to Freedom

In 1815, Truth married a farm labourer, Robert, and the pair had a daughter. However, in 1817, her owner, Dumont, forced her to marry an older man, Thomas, with whom she had two more daughters and a son.

In 1826, she escaped from Dumont with one of her daughters, but had to leave her other children behind. Later she managed to find her son Peter in Alabama – he had been illegally sold. She challenged the sale, and won her case. Sadly, Peter was lost at sea in the early 1840s.

Truth came to make one of the most momentous and famous speeches in 1851 at the Ohio Women's Rights Convention. Despite her illiteracy, and thanks to those who recorded her words, this speech continues to amaze and move us to the present day.

# The Ohio Women's Rights Convention of 1851

The Ohio Women's Rights Convention aimed to challenge conventional arguments against women as well as entrenched concepts of the inferiority of women due to physical and spiritual weakness.

Angus Calder and Lizbeth Goodman, in *Gender and Poetry*, describe the scene as Sojourner Truth delivered a diatribe that must have been shocking as well as unexpected.

Sojourner Truth: *"…stood up and literally bared her breast to the assembled public, showing her female form in an act of demonstration that she – and by extension, other African American women – are as female as white women, and are also strong, capable, remarkable…"*

(Points that Truth made in her speech were, allegedly, punctuated by her rallying cry: *"Ain't I a Woman!"* However, there have been different versions of the speech reproduced which are contradictory, and not all of them contain that phrase, or else, do not repeat it several times.)

# Addressing Issues of Sexism and Racism

Truth emphasised the fact that no one expected black women to be weak, because being slaves, they were usually strong in both a moral and a physical sense. In this way, Truth managed to combine issues both of sexism and racism because

*"white women counted, black women didn't."*

Truth insisted that society should acknowledge the rights of black women equally with those of white women, otherwise nothing would change for black women – their men would remain their masters and everything would stay the same.
She challenged the idea that women were inferior because Christ was a man.

*"Where did Christ come from,"* she demands, and in answer to her own question, she cries:

*"From God and a woman. Man had nothing to do with it."*

## The Early Feminists Endorse Dualism

Many early feminists preferred to stress the rational power of the female mind and regarded the body, as described in Kathleen Lennon's *"Feminine Perspectives on the Body"* as

*"a contingent characteristic of the self, and the potentially rational mind as its core."*

However, explains Lennon, Truth's speech at the Ohio Convention

*"drew attention to the body as a marker of race and class differences within the feminist movement."*

The position of black women justified acknowledgement, and Truth demanded that recognition in these eloquent words:

*"I have as much muscle as any man, and can do as much work as any man. I have ploughed, and planted, and gathered into barns, and no man could head me! And ain't I a woman? I could work as much and eat as much as a man—when I could get it—and bear de lash as well! And ain't I a woman?"*

## Sojourner Truth's Legacy

Truth spent her life passionately pursuing her causes such as land grants for former slaves. She was an opponent of capital punishment and a champion of desegregation of street-cars.

*Sojourner Truth's Biography* states:

*"Although she began her career as an abolitionist, the reform causes she sponsored were broad and varied including prison reform, property rights and universal suffrage. Abolition was one of the few causes that Truth was able to see realized in her lifetimes."*

Sojourner Truth died in her home in Michigan in 1883.

The Constitutional Amendment which forbade discrimination based on sex was not ratified until 37 years after her death, in 1920.

# Chapter 6

# Ernestine Rose, Activist and Philosopher
# The Queen of the Platform

39 Marine Parade, Brighton, East Sussex, UK,
where Ernestine Rose retired and where she died.
Image by Janet Cameron, all rights reserved.

Ernestine Potowski was born in Piotrknow, Poland, on 23 January, 1810; the daughter of a rabbi. She was passionate about social reform and humanitarian activities, and like many pioneering women, she was vulnerable to much abuse as well as gratitude for her great services.

Ernestine's mother died when she was just six years old, and; as a result, she endured a rigid childhood, as her father was a strict and strong-willed man… But nothing could crush Ernestine Rose's indomitable spirit.

## Conflict with Rabbi Father Over "Heresies"

*"About Ernestine Rose,"* published by *The Society of Ernestine Rose,* (author unnamed) describes Ernestine Rose's approach to religious studies:

*"Her intelligence was more given to questioning than accepting received wisdom."*

Ernestine's independence of thought during her studies of Judaism and the Talmud with her father caused a great rift between them.

*"Her goal for society was intellectual freedom, freedom from the constraints of religious creeds and dogma…She concluded that all major religions were both irrational and oppressive to women,"* explains *The Society of Ernestine Rose.*

At sixteen, her father betrothed Ernestine to a man much older than herself, but she refused him. When her father married a girl around Ernestine's own age, it became too much for her to bear, and she left home. She had to endure a legal battle for her mother's inheritance, and at the same time, she was obliged to defend herself from being sued by the rejected suitor.

## Ernestine Rose – Ever True to Herself

For a while Ernestine Rose lived in Berlin, although she had to fight for entry, as there were restrictions on Jewish immigrants. Then she travelled to France and Holland, and finally came to England in 1829 (in some sources, 1830) to teach languages. Ernestine was a creative and resourceful woman – she also marketed perfumed paper for use in crowded accommodation.

At no time did she consider converting from Judaism to Christianity, in spite of the pressure to do so, as many Jews did simply to make their lives more bearable. *About Ernestine Rose* quotes her as saying,

*"Shall I leave the tree to join a branch?"*

## Joined in a Common Purpose

In London, she met William Rose, a jeweller, and they married in a civil ceremony. They moved to New York in 1836 and this is where Ernestine's campaigning life began. It was a fine, mutually beneficial arrangement, as they were both equally committed to humanitarian goals and also cared deeply for one another.

William provided the stability and the financial support, while Ernestine honed her knowledge and her skills in the art of oratory. She spoke bravely against slavery, despite violent opposition.

W.J. McIlroy in his pamphlet, *Without the Faith, Freethinkers and Freethought in Brighton and Hove,* says:

*"An eloquent orator of indomitable courage, she denounced slavery at a time when Christian churches in that country were still defending it as a divine institution."*

## Helping the Under-Privileged

Both William and Ernestine followed the theories of Robert Owen, a rich industrialist who cared deeply about social and community issues. Owen and the Roses believed that the only way forward was to try to improve the condition of the poor, rather than blaming them for the results of their deprivation, as a judgmental society was prone to do.

In 1836, Ernestine Rose petitioned for the cause of married women's property rights and after twelve years of her activism, in 1848, New York State passed the first married women's property law in the United States of America.

The New York campaign led to connections between a number of great feminist activists and philosophers, among them Elizabeth Cady Stanton, Paulina Wright Davis and, eventually, in 1832, the well-known feminist, Susan B. Anthony.

## 'Worse Than a Common Prostitute'

W.J. McIlroy explains how Ernestine was also passionately committed to the cause of gender equality. A woman prepared to speak against slavery and gender-inequality, as well as being Jewish, an atheist and an abolitionist, went violently against the conformist society in which she lived.

According to McIlroy, *"…One newspaper described her as a "female atheist… a thousand times below a prostitute."*

## The Ernestine Rose Lectures

Fortunately, we know about Ernestine's great work since a number of her lectures were published. Her words are arousing and inspiring. You will find one in the resources at the end of this book, if you would like to read it for yourself.

When speaking of freedom, for example, from, *A Lecture in Women's Rights,* October 19, 1851, her metaphor is memorable in its strength and thrust:

*"The love of liberty has convulsed the nations like the mighty throes of an earthquake."*

In the same lecture, pertaining to women's rights, she says,

*"WOMAN is rising, in the full dignity of her being, to claim the recognition of her rights."*

It is not clear whether the capitals are hers as written, or whether they are there to indicate the emphasis she placed on the word. Either way, it imparts to the word an urgency for which most of society wasn't entirely prepared.

As for her atheism, McIlroy quotes from one of these lectures, controversially entitled *In Defence of Atheism:*

*"You ask how it is that Man talked or wrote about God. The answer is very simple. Ignorance is the mother of superstition. In proportion to Man's ignorance, he is very superstitious."*

## An Iconoclastic Figure, Forgotten by History

It is extraordinary that a woman of such courage, ability and confidence, and who made such enormous humanitarian changes and improvements, is not better known today. *The Society of Ernestine Rose* says:

*"Though Rose's early and continuing contribution to the advance of women's rights is unquestionable, her social status may have contributed to the lack of recognition from historians. She was an immigrant in a period of rising nativist sentiment, a Jew in largely Protestant reform movements, a freethinker and atheist in movements that often turned to the Bible for authority."*

It seems a poor legacy to be so neglected for a woman whose rallying cry was

*"LIBERTY, EQUALITY, FRATERNITY."*

Women, everywhere, must be thankful for her sacrifices and her contributions, and must work to ensure she takes her rightful place in the history books.

Ernestine Rose died at her home in 39 Marine Parade, Brighton, on 4 August 1892 and is buried in Highgate Cemetery in London together with the husband she loved.

# Chapter 7

# Ada Lovelace: Philosopher of Science and First Computer Programmer

Ada Lovelace, computer programming pioneer.
Image courtesy of the Science and Society
Picture Library.

Ada Lovelace (1815-1852), the only daughter of poet George Gordon, Lord Byron, never saw her father. Byron abandoned baby Ada and her young mother, Anne Isabelle Millibanke, 11th Baroness Wentworth, and left England forever when the child was just four months old.

According to the *Finding Ada* organisation, Ada's mother feared:

*"Ada would inherit her father's volatile 'poetic' temperament,"* and as a result, *"…raised her under a strict regimen of science, logic, and mathematics."*

In his article, *"Ada Lovelace, on how a poet's daughter invented the concept of software,"* Sir Alistair MacFarlane, a former Vice-President of the Royal Society and a retired university Vice-Chancellor, explains how Lovelace derived inspiration for her incredible insights from the work of Charles Babbage, Lucasian Professor of Mathematics.

Babbage designed his Analytical Engine for the sole purpose of making simple mathematical calculations, an advancement on his Difference Engine.

## The World's First Computer Programmer

Ada Lovelace, who described herself as an Analyst and Metaphysician, translated a description of the Analytical Engine written in French by an Italian mathematician named Luigi Menabrea. Her understanding of the material appeared to equal that of Charles Babbage, but she was apparently better able to articulate its import and envision its potential.

She responded that surely, such an invention could be used to produce music, providing the application of a suitable set of rules. Merry Maisel and Laura Smart of the San Diego Supercomputer Center quote Lovelace's actual assessment:

*"It was suited for developping (sic) and tabulating any function whatever…. the engine [is] the material expression of any indefinite function of any degree of generality and complexity."*

MacFarlane says,

*"Lovelace realised that such a device could be set to execute any logically coherent series of instructions, and in this she became the world's first computer programmer."*

However, more than this, Lovelace was able to predict that the development of the Analytical Engine would far exceed that of mere data processing.

## Roll Over Beethoven!

Ada Lovelace's predictions were incredibly visionary, especially for the time in which she lived, and they were stunning in their accuracy. In her notes on Babbage's article, *"Sketch of the Analytical Engine Invented by Charles Babbage,"* she says:

"[The Analytical Engine] *might act upon other things besides numbers… Supposing, for instance, that the fundamental relations of pitched sounds in the science of harmony and of musical composition were susceptible of such expression and adaptation, the engine might compose elaborate and scientific pieces of music of any degree or complexity or extent."*

When she was writing the first computer programme about Bernoulli Numbers, a highly-complex sequence of rational numbers with deep connections to number theory, she said:

*"I'm a devil or an angel. I'm working like a devil for you, Charles Babbage. I'm sifting the Bernoulli numbers."*

Her work on Bernoulli Numbers became the first computer programme, claims Dr. Betty Toole, who wrote *Ada, The Enchantress of Numbers,* and who, in an online interview, adds:

*"She saw the nature of the machine…. that it could compose music, that it could do graphics, and that it could show science in ways we never, ever could conceive of. She was a prophet."*

## The Genius and Vision of the Enchantress of Numbers

Between them, Ada Lovelace and Charles Babbage are responsible for the eventual modern technical marvel, computer software. Alistair MacFarlane heaps high praise on Ada Lovelace's contribution, made possible through her personal vision, or what MacFarlane describes as her "*prescience*"; in other words, her foreknowledge about events that had not taken place and for which she had no model.

He says, *"Leonardo da Vinci had anticipated the development of flying machines by several centuries, but he had the advantage of having seen birds flying. What puts Ada Lovelace's prescience in an altogether higher class, is that she had grasped how to make physical instantiations of <u>wholly abstract concepts</u>."*

Our modern-day computer hardware could not perform its tasks without the software in place, and we can only imagine, how in 1842, this achievement must have seemed miraculous, and *was*, in fact, miraculous.

*"She thus anticipated the development of both modern computer <u>and</u> artificial intelligence by more than 100 years,"* says MacFarlane.

Ada Lovelace helped set the stage
for the modern computer.
Image courtesy of NASA.

According to the *Finding Ada* organization, Babbage described her as:

*"that Enchantress who has thrown her magical spell around the most abstract of the Sciences, and has grasped it with a force that few masculine intellects could have exerted over it."*

## "My Brain is More Than Mortal, As Time Will Show"

Rowan Hooper, in his article *"Ada Lovelace: My brain is more than merely mortal,"* describes how she moves easily from the specific in her work, to the universal.

Lovelace says, *"It may be desirable to explain that, by the word operation, we mean any process which alters mutual relations of two or more things…. [this] would include all subjects in the universe."*

She insists the science of operations derived from mathematics is a science in itself with its own *"abstract truth."*

Yet she was also matter-of-fact about her insights.

*"We may say most aptly that the Analytical Engine weaves algebraic patterns just as the Jacquard loom weaves leaves and flowers."*

## Ada Lovelace Day

There is even an Ada Lovelace Day, intended to *"raise the profile of great women in science, technology, engineering and mathematics by encouraging people around the world to talk about the women whose work they admire."* Suw Charman-Anderson founded the special day, held on 15 October each year. Science, technology, engineering and mathematics are now known as the STEM subjects.

The truth is that, claims psychologist Penny Lockspeed for the *Finding Ada* organisation, *"women need to see female role models more than male role models. Without female role models they are deprived of the inspiration to overcome gender barriers and discover their true potential."*

## The Highest Level of Scientific Achievement and Philosophical Insight

Sadly, Ada Lovelace's life was a short one and she died at just 36 of uterine cancer. During her life, she suffered a number of illnesses, which she ignored, living her life to the fullest, even attracting scandal through her love affairs and her gambling. Ada's debts on her death amounted to around £2000. MacFarlane succinctly sums up her legacy:

*"Ada Lovelace's abiding legacy is that, despite all the obstacles in her path, she demonstrated beyond any possibility of doubt that women could attain the highest levels of scientific understanding and achievement… This sudden understanding of the immense possibilities opened up by programmable computers may never be equalled for prophetic insight."*

MacFarlane further expresses his hope that there will be more opportunities for aspiring women scientist and philosophers, so that

*"another such meteor of great insight will flash across the sky."*

In 1979, a software package developed by the U.S. Department of Defense was named "Ada" in her honour.

# CHAPTER 8

# Elizabeth Cady Stanton, (1815-1902): Activist, Abolitionist, Feminist

Elizabeth Cady Stanton (seated)
and Susan B. Anthony (standing).
Image by the U.S. Library of Congress

Critics scathingly called a statue depicting three suffragettes the *"Three Ladies in a Bathtub."*

The three American suffragettes comprising the 7.5 ton *Portrait Monument* are Elizabeth Cady Stanton, Lucretia Mott and Susan B. Anthony, who led the great political battle for the right to vote in the United States of America. However, the government had abandoned the statue in the Capitol basement before returning it to the rotunda in 1997.

*"It took a special act of Congress, passed at the urging of the women's groups, who believed the pioneer suffragettes deserved better than the capitol basement,"* says the Louise Schiavone in her article, *"Even in stone, suffragettes cause a stir on Capitol Hill."*

The statue had been installed in the rotunda in 1921, but an all-male Congress removed it; a shameful act regarding what Joan Meacham, co-chair of The Women's Suffrage Campaign, describes as

*"The greatest bloodless revolution in the history of the country."*

## The Beginning of Women's Suffrage in America

The American Women's suffrage movement began in 1848, (although English activists did not follow the example of the American women until 1876).

Lizbeth Goodman in her chapter, *"Gender and drama, text and performance,"* says:

*"The struggle for the vote for women was fought for many years in the United States alongside the Civil Rights Movement. Sojourner Truth's words were often cited as a parallel between the situation of women and African-Americans in their disfranchized status: 'if colored men get their rights and not colored women theirs, you see (sic) the colored men will be masters over the women and it will be just as bad as it was before.'"*

Sojourner Truth was the illiterate African-American woman whose passionate cry *"Ain't I a Woman"* was later taken up by such great writers as Alice Walker and Maya Angelou.

The two movements fought alongside each other for many years.

## The Father who Wanted a Son

When we consider Elizabeth Cady Stanton's early life, and the issues she had to confront, it seems fitting that she became a pioneer for women's rights. She was born in Johnstown, New York, in 1815 and *A&E TV Network's* website *"bio"* records that her lawyer father had wanted a son. This must have had a profound effect on the young daughter, because it compelled her to try to excel in all traditionally-male areas of expertise.

Young Elizabeth received her education at Johnstown Academy, Troy Female Seminary. She had a cousin who was also an activist, Gerrit Smith, and visits to his home influenced her views.

In 1840, Elizabeth Cady Stanton met Henry Stanton and agreed to marry him, but she insisted that the minister omit the word "obey" from the marriage oath. In view of the time in which she lived, this was a momentous stand for a woman to take, and it is to the credit of her husband that he agreed. The couple became parents to seven children, yet still she managed to pursue her energetic activist philosophy.

## The Seneca Falls Conference, 1848

Elizabeth Cady Stanton and fellow-activist, Lucretia Mott, were both involved in the movement to abolish slavery. However, Lucretia Mott had been forbidden to speak at the World Anti-Slavery Convention in London because she was a woman – even though she was an official delegate.

The two women called the Conference at Seneca Falls to address issues of women's rights, as set out by Paul Halsall in his article "The Declaration of Sentiments:"

*"The Declaration of the Seneca Falls Convention, using the model of the US Declaration of Independence, forthrightly demanded that the rights of women as right-bearing individuals be acknowledged and respected by society. It was signed by sixty-eight women and thirty-two men."*

## An Alliance with Susan B. Anthony

In the 1850s, Elizabeth Cady Stanton met Susan B. Anthony (1820-1906) and the two women co-founded the National Woman Suffrage Association (later to become the League of Women Voters.)  In 1868, they worked on a militant weekly paper called *Revolution*.

American government officials continued to thwart their efforts to improve women's rights. The Nineteenth Amendment, popularly known's as the "Anthony Amendment," calling for equal rights for women in respect of voting, hit a brick wall.

Lizbeth Goodman's says:

*"In 1878 however, the Anthony amendment was blocked and at every subsequent Congressional Session right up until the 26 August 1920, when the Amendment was finally ratified."*

Congress passed the Nineteenth Amendment in June, 1919 and was finally ratified on 18 August 1920. This is the wording of the Amendment as set in *"Women's Fight for the Vote"* on the website *"Exploring Constitutional Conflicts."*

*"Section 1: The right of citizens of the United States to vote shall not be denied or abridged by the United States or by any State on account of sex.*

*Section 2: Congress shall have power to enforce this article by appropriate legislation."*

## Fearless and Uncompromising

Elizabeth Cady Stanton is an incredible icon, not only for her intense commitment to her causes, but for the wide range of issues she addressed. Occasionally, her beliefs even upset other suffragettes, less free-thinking, or maybe just less courageous, than she was.

Stanton campaigned for the right for women to ride bicycles.

She criticised the Bible and organised religion for their part in the oppression of women, and with her daughter Harriet Stanton Blatch, she wrote "*The Woman's Bible.*" She also wrote a history of the suffragette movement with Susan B. Anthony.

Elizabeth Cady Stanton was both fearless and uncompromising – and women the world over owe her a great debt of gratitude.

# Chapter 9

# Ayn Rand Challenges Hume's Guillotine

This is the cover of Ayn Rand's 'Philosophy: Who Needs It,' which includes Raphael's 'The School of Athens.' Image courtesy of 1Veertje.

Radical thinker Ayn Rand is an unconventional and controversial philosopher who described her philosophy as "objectivism."

Ayn Rand (1905-1982) was born in St. Petersburg in Russia, and studied at the University of Petrograd (as St. Petersburg was named then) although later she took on American citizenship. She came to America in 1925, where she first earned her living as a screenwriter, and later as a novelist; integrating radical ideas into her famous novels, *The Fountainhead* and *Atlas Shrugged.*

Rand's philosophy is essentially straightforward.  In *Atlas Shrugged*, Part I, Chapter VII, Rand has one of her characters say:

*"Contradictions do not exist. Whenever you think that you are facing a contradiction, check your premises. You will find that one of them is wrong."*

## Accused of Making a Virtue out of Selfishness

Critics have accused Rand of making a virtue of selfishness. These are the central tenets of Ayn Rand's objectivism:

- Individual happiness is the highest human aspiration.
- Work and achievement are the highest human goals.
- Everything should be privately run, although if force is required, governments may intervene.
- A free-market system is the only moral system.
- Self-sacrifice is immoral.

Rand says that existence exists, therefore objective reality exists, independent of any perceiver, or the perceiver's feelings.

For Ayn Rand, reason is the only way to perceive reality.

A painting of David Hume (1754) by Allan Ramsey, courtesy of the
Scottish National Portrait Gallery. Image by Guinnog.

Hume's Guillotine: You Cannot Derive "Ought" from "Is"

So – what is Ayn Rand up against in challenging the tricky concept of Hume's Guillotine?

Hume's Guillotine is also known as Hume's Law, or, alternatively, as the *"is/ought* question;" it appears in *The Treatise of Human Nature, Book III.*

An "ought" statement is known as a "normative" statement. However, we cannot use "ought" as the conclusion of reason, says Hume.

In other words, we cannot derive "ought" from "is" in order to make a moral valuation from a factual statement. How can we say an argument is valid because things should be different from how they are?

An example of the argument Hume rejects might be as follows:

1. Children cry if you speak sharply to them.
2. Gemma is a child. Therefore

3. You should not speak sharply to Gemma.

> This is not a valid argument as the first two premises do not necessarily make the third option logical. You might agree with the first two options, but supposing Gemma is distracted and about to run into the road. She might be run over, so is it logical to speak to her gently so she doesn't hear the urgency of the statement? How can you make a moral logical conclusion about this predicament.

So Hume's Guillotine is a metaphor for the severance of "ought" from "is." One cannot logically follow the other. The fact that something "is" can't presuppose that something "ought" to be. This is because the "ought" is not derived from the "is" – but from the goal itself, which is, essentially, "the ought."

## Ayn Rand's Argument Against Hume's "Atilla-ism"

Morality, for Rand, needs to be shown to operate independently of the human will. As she makes clear in *The Virtue of Selfishness,* she hates terms relating morality to irrationality, for example, subjective choice, emotional commitments, or "whim." Instead, she defines morality and ethics as follows:

*"What is morality, or ethics? It is a code of values to guide man's choices and actions – the choices and actions that determine the purpose and course of his life. Ethics, as a science, deals with discovering and defining such a code."*

She disputes Aristotle's statement that ethics is not an exact science, believing instead, that a proper moral system is capable of being rational. As for Hume, she describes his scepticism as *"Atilla-ism"* which, O'Neill claims, is hardly unfair of her since *"power is the overall determinant."*

Is Rand unfair in making such a forceful and negative claim against David Hume?

In *The Virtue of Selfishness,* Rand begins her argument by pointing out:
*"The concept "value" is not a primary. It presupposes an answer to the questions "to whom?" or "for what?"*

Then, she establishes a link between life as value, by using a character, John Galt, from her novel *Atlas Shrugged.* John Galt says that only living entities can have values and that the great fundamental alternatives in the cosmos are existence and non-existence.

In the end, Rand reaches the conclusion that this organism, life itself, is its own standard of value. She claims that it is a phenomenon that is "*an end in itself*." Therefore, the role of value is in preserving life and injecting meaning into it. We avoid subjectivity because the "choice" is "chosen" correctly.

O'Neill says that Rand then contradicts herself and falls metaphorically under the Guillotine, when she states that what a human *is* decides what it *ought* to do. O'Neill says,

*"Clearly Rand thinks that Hume denied a connection between fact and systems of morality. The error is not uncommon."*

In essence, David Hume's argument was not that value and morality cannot be integrated. His claim was only that a value could not be derived, logically, from a statement of fact. It is purely an argument of reason, not a statement of how we should live.

## Iris Murdoch – On the Instinctive Connection of Fact with Value

Hume is actually easy-going about combining fact with value. As we have seen, through his Guillotine, he is merely objecting to the deriving of values from facts. Hume is presenting an argument of reason. As Iris Murdoch says in her book *Metaphysics as a Guide to Morals,*

*"…he wants no drama made of this since habit and custom and semi-reflective feelings are not only the best but the only available guides to conduct. This, in effect, allows an instinctive, if not intellectual connection of fact with value."*

The key word here is "instinctive."

Hume accepts and celebrates our instincts to passion and feeling.

Later, in her *Metaphysics as a Guide to Morals*, Murdoch says,

*"…he means that reason is bound, one way or another, whether we like it, or admit it, or not, to be swayed, or coloured, by desires; and moreover this is a good thing…"*

## Ayn Rand's Objectivism – What is it Good For?

There are a few positive outcomes from Rand's objectivism since it encourages responsibility and upholds the constitutional protection of human rights in respect of freedom and property. Objectivism also limits the powers of government, which may be a good thing in certain situations, although maybe not in others.

However, for most people, it is desperately lacking in moderation and empathy.

# Chapter 10

# Hannah Arendt Addresses Adolf Eichmann's Culpability: The Banality of Evil

Hannah Arendt, 1906-1975.
Image courtesy of wpclipart.

Hannah Arendt (1906-1975), born in Hanover, was an influential political philosopher whose commitment to upholding fundamental human rights, absolutely without reservation, exposed her to condemnation and personal angst. She preferred being known as a political theorist.

She was once a student of the great existentialist German philosopher, Martin Heidegger (1889-1976). Arendt was a Jew, and Heidegger exhibited sympathies for National Socialism, praising Hitler and joining the Nazi Party. Later, as his thinking changed, Heidegger withdrew his support from the regime, but this early involvement with the Nazis affected his career.

The two philosophers had a brief, but a passionate affair during their time together and remained friends.

## Totalitarianism and Nazi Terror

A totalitarian state is a one-party state that is dictatorial, and that regulates every aspect of life. The Nazis banned Arendt as a young activist from teaching in Germany and she fled from her country to escape persecution.

As soon as the Germans invaded France, the French interred Arendt in Gurs, a concentration camp. Many women remained incarcerated, but Arendt managed to escape.

After this experience, and her knowledge of the terrors of Stalin in Soviet Russia, Arendt believed that these totalitarian regimes were pure political evil, and that terror was no longer a means to an end, but an end in itself.

*The New Yorker* commissioned Hannah Arendt to write a series of articles covering Adolf Eichmann's trial in Jerusalem for crimes against humanity. The articles and her subsequent book exposed her to accusations of betraying the Jews – her own people.

## Can 'Thinking' Condition us Against Doing Evil?

In her assessment of the character of Adolf Eichmann, Arendt concluded that he was not capable of self-judgment and he was unaware of the nature of his deeds.

He simply did not think about it, but obeyed orders, considering it his duty to obey orders above all other things.

Judith Butler of the guardian.co says:

*"Her argument was that Eichmann may well have lacked 'intentions' insofar as he failed to think about the crime he was committing. She did not think he acted without conscious activity, but she insisted that the term "thinking" had to be reserved for a more reflective mode of rationality."*

Is it mitigation for his crime to claim that Eichmann didn't think? He was ordinary. He was a bureaucrat. He maintained he had no argument with the Jews, that he was not anti-semitic. He was merely carrying out his duty to the Reich.

## The Fine Line Between Resistance and Cooperation

Arendt asks searching and difficult questions. She maintains:
*"Thinking and reason are not mutually exclusive. People believe reason and passion are opposites… What about passionate thinking? There can be such a thing as passionate thinking."*

She points out that in the Eichmann case, history itself was not being tried, but the deeds of just one man.

## Non-Thinking is Banal, Even Though the Deed is Shocking

Judith Butler says:

*"To have 'intentions' in her view was to think reflectively about one's own action as a political being, whose own life and thinking is bound up with the life and thinking of others… she feared that what had become 'banal' was non-thinking itself. This fact was not banal at all, but unprecedented, shocking, and wrong."*

Arendt was not even campaigning against the death penalty for Eichmann. She firmly believed he should hang, that it was his due. This did not seem a contradiction to her in view of her assessment of this infamous war criminal.

However, this was not just a crime against the Jews, explains Judith Butler.

Arendt needed to *"…understand a crime against humanity, one that would acknowledge the destruction of Jews, Gypsies, gay people, communists, the disabled and the ill… [the] destruction and displacement of whole populations was an attack not only on those specific groups, but on humanity itself… the crime had become for the criminals accepted, routinised, and implemented without moral revulsion and political indignation and resistance."*

A Jewish mother and children going to the gas chamber.
Image courtesy of German Federal Archives;
Bundesarchiv, Bild 183-74237-004 / CC-BY-SA.

Arendt became the subject of much criticism, even abuse, for her theories about Eichmann. Many roundly rejected her reasoning, while others acknowledged the concept – that evil could, indeed, be banal – but that Eichmann's case was a poor example.

## The Jewish Magazine Responds to Arendt's Theory of Banality

Laurence Rosenberg presents us with an alternative concept of banality. (although this particular example might seem more an argument stemming from ignorance, since a small child could know nothing of the actual consequences of his action.)

*"An analogy – a poor one at that – might be that of a six year-old boy pushing buttons on a brightly colored console that launches nuclear weapons. The human damage would be great but the act really could not be considered an evil one."*

Rosenberg maintains that Arendt's assessment of Eichmann's inability to understand the consequences of his actions is naïve.

*"Here was a man who climbed very high…in the government; he must have possessed… political savvy to have engineered such a feat… who walked into the offices of the European emperors and prime ministers and asked them to deport their loyal, taxpaying citizens; he would have seemed quite a fool if he truly had no idea where they were going and conveyed that ignorance. My guess is that he was playing a role in that Jerusalem courtroom; he was acting the innocent – and yes, perhaps, the buffoon – as if to thumb his nose at the Jews and their system of justice."*

## Holocaust Same as Everyday Life except in Scale

Rosenberg insists Eichmann expressed no regret because he had none, that he was a clever man with low self-esteem. Thoughtlessness is not needed to prove the validity of banality.

*"Thoughtlessness is just one cause of evil behaviour."*

Acts of the holocaust, says Rosenberg, are the same as those in everyday life.

*"What made the holocaust distinct was its scale and genocidal intent; it was different in degree but not in kind from the everyday, human phenomena of evil actions. Moreover, if one were able to recreate similar conditions, something similar could happen again."*

## The Worst Evil is a Senseless Existence

Arendt, however, maintains that the worst evil is not selfishness.

The worst evil is *senselessness*, when people feel there is no meaning to their life. It is about making humans unnecessary. It is when work produces no results. It is senseless activity, so that life and self-worth mean nothing.

She also examines why people were so easily taken in by Totalitarianism and concludes:

*"...it offered a single clear and unambiguous idea to a disenchanted and disaffected people that accounted for their present woes and promised them a future free from danger and insecurity."*

# CHAPTER 11

# Simone de Beauvoir: Feminist, Philosopher, Trailblazer

Simone de Beauvoir says individual
freedom requires the freedom of
others in order to be recognised.
Image courtesy of WP Clipart.

Feminist, philosopher and trailblazer,Simone de Beauvoir (1908-1986) met with her soul mate, Jean-Paul Sartre while they were both students. The two philosophers now share a grave in the Montparnesse Cemetery in Paris, France, after a lifetime of companionship. De Beauvoir was a pioneer, unrelenting in her pursuit of women's rights and emancipation.

De Beauvoir became the youngest philosophy teacher at the Sorbonne after passing her final examination at the age of 21 years. She made significant philosophical contributions in the field of ethics from an existentialist viewpoint, insisting upon the individual's ethical responsibility for him/herself and for others – for example those who are economically and socially oppressed.

## The Power of the Individual

Existentialism is about the power of the individual; it claims that it's not enough to rely on moral and/or scientific thinking in order to become a fully-realised human being. At all times, a person must be true to themselves.

Her book, *The Second Sex,* published in 1948, focused on female oppression in all its guises. It undermined and challenged gender issues that were limiting and that denied women the right of self-determination. The strength of her commitment evoked wide-ranging criticism from both the right and left, and offended the Vatican who showed its disapproval by listing her book in their *Index of Prohibited Books.*

## Simone de Beauvoir and the *Eternal Feminine*

In *The Second Sex*, we are introduced to the concept of woman being termed as "The Other" by men, thereby labeling her as inessential. According to this concept, man is "Subject" and "Absolute" making relationships between male and female unequal.

De Beauvoir decided to uncover the roots of this inequality, and to expose attitudes that helped to maintain the *status quo,* causing woman to live in a manner considered appropriate for her by men. There were certain requirements that needed to be recognized, if women were to emancipate themselves.

*"A modern woman prides herself on thinking, taking action, working, creating, on the same terms as men; instead of seeking to disparage them, she declares herself their equal."*

To achieve this the following changes were necessary, according to Jeremy Harwood, in *Great Thinkers.*

- The instigation of change in the existing social structure.
- The provision of universal childcare.
- Equality in education.
- Contraception and the legalisation of abortion.
- Women's economic freedom and independence from men.

Passerelle Simone de Beauvoir.
A cycle and footbridge across the
River Seine in Paris, named for
France's great woman philosopher.
Image by Dinkum.

## The Vanity of Women Limits Their Power

In her book, *The New Feminism,* Natasha Walter says, *"Feminists down the ages have argued that the oppression of women is played out on their bodies, their clothes, their styles of adornment. To politicize dress has been one of the enduring projects of the women's movement."*

Walter quotes Mary Wollstonecraft, who said, in 1792, that women were *"…confined in cages like the feathered race… nothing to do but plume themselves… stalk from perch to perch."*

In this way women, it was claimed, became the object of men's sexual desires rather than independent individuals…

*"thus society is not seeking to further her projects but to thwart them."*

Natasha Walter cites several examples of how women's dress has been used against them, for example, beauty contests, make-up, hair-dye, so that she appears to be permanently on display. In Simone de Beauvoir's words,

*"What is decorated is what is offered."*

## The Root of the Problem is Not Vanity

However, Walter has a different angle of this viewpoint. She feels such issues are rooted in the fact of financial inequality between the sexes.
*"… men indulge their narcissism in ceremonial dress – the curling wigs of judges, the bright livery of the Horse Guards, the purple dresses of bishops, the stiff shirts of empire builders at dinner…"*

Walter insists that providing our dress does not stop us from *"doing things"* (as crinolines might) we should not attribute such concepts to it.

*"Narcissism by the ruling group will always be seen as powerful, narcissism by subordinates as demeaning,"* she says.

Although later feminists, like Natasha Walter, declare that de Beauvoir's message is misguided because it postulates that women should become more like men, this is not entirely fair. Jeremy Harwood says:

*"...nowhere did de Beauvoir say that male qualities are superior to female ones. What she did say is that only be achieving those ends can women become liberated."*

## Simone de Beauvoir – Midwife of Sartre's Existentialism

It is, perhaps, a little ironic that, according to the *Stanford Encyclopedia of Philosophy*, de Beauvoir described herself as the *"midwife of Sartre's existentialism"* rather than a thinker in her own right. When she died on 14 April 1986, she was famous for her support of women's rights and as a writer, but not as a philosopher. The reason for this was because not only did she write about women, not a pressing philosophical issue during her lifetime, but because readers considered her work to be "echoes" of that of Jean-Paul Sartre.

In truth, she was very much a thinker in her own right and fully familiar with the work of Leibniz, Hegel, Husserl, Heidegger, Marx, Descartes and Bergson.

Another key work of de Beauvoir's was *The Ethics of Ambiguity*. She described her philosophical approach as *"combining literature and metaphysics."*

# Chapter 12

# Simone Weil: Love is the Intermediary Between Us and the Divine

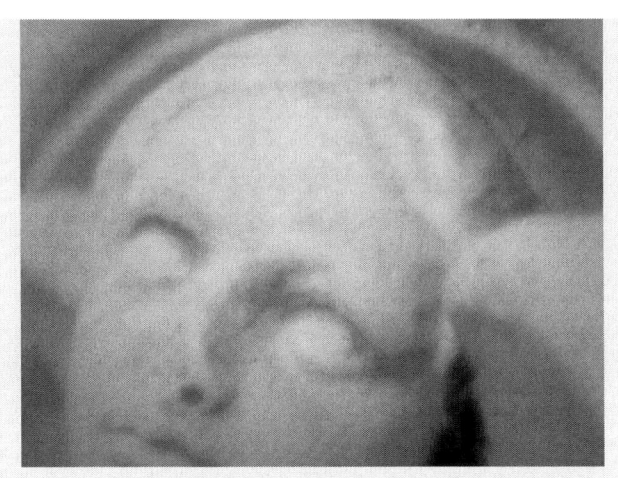

Simone Weil believed God took
possession of her as she listened to poetry.
Image by Janet Cameron.

Simone Weil's life was tragically short. This uniquely gifted woman was born into an agnostic Jewish family in 1909, although later she became a committed and devout Christian.

During her lifetime, Weil never went to a synagogue, and claimed she had no connection with Judaism as a religion. She died of tuberculosis in 1943.

She was the daughter of a physician who forbade her to become a doctor herself, and the presence of her gifted brother, who was three years older, further diminished her. Simone Weil published a number of poems and articles, although it was not until after her death, that the public recognised her originality and genius.

Plato's work greatly influenced Simone Weil and she was antagonistic toward Descartes.

## Spiritual and Political Labelling

The poet, T.S. Eliot, describes Weil as:

*"a woman of genius – akin to that of the saints."*
She endured another *"label"* in her early youth, and one rather less complimentary than T.S. Eliot's, that of *"The Red Virgin."* Later, she turned her back on communism due to its inherent bureaucracy. Her name for herself was *"The Platonic Christian,"* which elegantly sums up the strength of her faith and her spiritual mysticism. Her Christian belief was close to that of Catholicism, and she was also a woman with a strong sense of political purpose, social justice and moral idealism.

After the Russian Revolution, a classmate accused her of being a Communist, and she answered: *"Not at all; I am a Bolshevik."*

## An Acute Empathy for the Suffering of Others

At aged six years, or in some sources, five years, Simone Weil empathised so deeply with the soldiers of the First World War that she refused to eat sugar, because they had none. She limited her own food so that it equalled soldiers' rations. Her empathy for others was frequently at her own expense.

Although a pacifist, she went to Spain, because she wanted to volunteer for the Republican side in the Civil War, and she supported the French resistance in England.

On the BBC Radio 4 programme, *In Our Time*, Steven Plant of the University of Cambridge, says, *"Her life and thoughts are illustrations each of the other."* In other words, Weil lived as she thought; her life and her thought fed upon each other.

She was, at various times in her life, a factory worker, a teacher and a political activist.

## The Nature of Truth and Goodness

The *In Our Time* philosophers discuss Weil's idea of what is truth. Truth, she says, is impersonal. Truth is not an opinion.

2×2=4… that is truth. The deepest truths have that quality of geometry.

Personal truths are different. Personal relationships, for example, may become corrupted… a corrupted imperfection, and therefore a distraction from God.

Plant says Weil has two Gods, a good God, and an evil God. She also has two religions, a good religion of mysticism and truth, and a bad religion that is false, nationalistic and self-assertive. Judaism, she claims, has much in common with this false, nationalistic religion. This element of her thought can seem disturbing, because she carries these views to extremes.

David Levy of the University of Edinburgh also mentions Weil's two kinds of *"good."* The first is *"Good in the World"* and the second is *"Absolute Good."* Absolute good is God's perfection. Weil reconciles the goodness of God in a world of suffering as follows:

*"She argued that the presence of evil and suffering in the world was evidence of God's love, and that Man had no right to ask anything of God, or of anyone whom they love. Love which expects rewards was not love at all in Weil's eyes."*

## How to Engage with God

Weil believes the realisation of truth is available to everyone, that human beings need to pay attention and truth will come to them. She is fond of telling a metaphor, says David Levy, that of a wall separating two prisoners who cannot communicate except by banging on the wall. In this way, they relate to each other, if imperfectly. In the same way as they are separated from each other, so are we separated from God, but He is accessible to us. We just need to *"bang on the wall."*

We engage the world by forms of the implicit love of God. Beauty, friendship, religious ceremonies – all these can lead Mankind to God.

## Simone Weil and "Unselfing"

Weil believes we have no will of our own. In her *Notebooks*, she speaks of the Zen method, quoted by Iris Murdoch.

*"The primitive Zen method seems to consist of a gratuitous search of such intensity that it takes the place of all attachments. But, because it is gratuitous, it cannot become an object of attachment in so far as it is actively pursued, and the activity involved in this fruitless search becomes exhausted. When exhaustion point has been almost reached, some shock or other brings about detachment."*

In the chapter *"Consciousness and Thought,"* in *Metaphysics as a Guide to Morals*, Iris Murdoch says of Weil:

*"The imageless austerity of Zen is impressive and attractive. It represents to us 'the real thing'; what it is like to be stripped of the ego and how different this is… Simone Weil felt a natural affinity with this extremism, which, indeed, she practised in her own life. She, at the same time, loved Plato and the mystical Christ."*

Simone Weil describes this distance as *decreation,* a form of un-selfing.

# Decreation

On the *In Our Time* programme, David Levy of the University of Edinburgh explains what Weil means when she speaks of decreation. This is a term with a specialised meaning. It relates to the act of creation. When God created us, He limited Himself, in his perfection and power, to *"create space for us."*

Therefore, if we decreate ourselves to some extent, we reverse some of that act of creation and, as a result, we come closer to God.

## Causes of Conflict

Weil committed herself to politics and political activism. Gary Goodwin in his *Registry of Mysticism* quotes from her work, *The Need for Roots,* 1949:

*"What a country calls its vital economic interests are not the things which enable its citizens to live, but the things which enable it to make war. Gasoline is much more likely than wheat to be a cause of international conflict."*

## Pain and Grief

For states of pain and grief which transcend mere unhappiness, she employs the term *"malheur."* Murdoch suggests this could be translated as *"affliction"* although there is no accurate translation into English. Most *"afflictions"* normally can be alleviated in some way. Malheur is something that demolishes the spirit, and leaves the human being with no relief and no hope.

However, paradoxically, Weil says that *malheur* can be a route to a knowledge of God. *In Our Time* explains how we can feel melancholy, for example, after a love affair has ended. This can lead us to becoming more lucid about our faults. In that moment, we may stop fooling ourselves and recognise that we are selfish or self-serving.

Murdoch quotes from Weil's Notebooks, Volume 2: *"…exposure to God condemns what's evil in us."*

## Weil's Mysticism – Three Profound Experiences

Simone Weil had three or four powerful, mystical experiences. She makes it plain, says Beatrice Han Pile, of Essex University, on the programme *In Our Time,* that she never sought God, but that He came to find her.

The first was at Assisi, when Weil felt a force so powerful and stronger than her will, so that she felt compelled to fall to her knees.

A year later, a further experience occurred while she was in a Benedictine Monastery. She had a terrible, splitting headache and had huddled in a corner, then she found herself leaving her miserable flesh and rising in accord with the music.

Another mystical happening was during a poetry recitation of George Herbert's poem, *"Love bade me welcome while my Soul drew back."* Weil reports that Christ came down and took possession of her.

Naturally, all these experience had a profound and lasting effect on Weil.

## Health Issues Lead to Mystical Experiences

Gary Goodwin explains how Simone Weil had many problems in her life, including an obsession with hand-washing which she imposed on her family due to a terrible fear of microbes. Outsiders were not permitted to kiss her children and she had difficulties with food beginning in her childhood.

As a result she suffered from malnutrition and it's suggested on the *Mystical Experience Registry* that this lack of food may have affected her brain and contributed to her mystical experiences.

It is also possible that they simply made her susceptible to such experiences.

## Obedience and Necessity

*"Simone Weil's obedience and necessity are better understood as a confrontation with what is not just unintelligible, but pointless,"* says Iris Murdoch.

Murdoch is saying that Weil is not trying to propel us towards moral improvement. She is focused mainly on the idea of obligations.

*"Moral change comes from an attention to the world whose natural result is a decrease in egoism through an increased sense of the reality of, of course, other people, but also other things."*

This, Murdoch explains, is close in meaning to Oriental wisdom – that, ultimately, as human beings, we have no will.

Levy quotes Weil's famous wisdom: *"To stop saying 'I' one needs to pay attention."*

# Chapter 13

# Philippa Foot Says
# Moral Philosophy Starts with Plants

Plants need strong roots to flourish.
Human beings need courage.

In an interview with Rick Lewis of *Philosophy Now*, moral philosopher Philippa Foot explains her theory about *'natural goodness,'* stating that vice is actually a form of natural defect.

We can describe defects in human beings in exactly the same way as we describe defects in plants and animals. It is, she claims, important to begin by discussing plants. *"This surprised some people!"* she says.

The surprise seems reasonable. After all, we, as human beings, are a good deal more complex than plants, as are many other species; and we are probably the only species able to question and evaluate its own motives.

Even those of us who talk to our plants, believing this benefits their growth and development, would not expect to learn how to become better people by communing with them on moral dilemmas.

## We Are As We Are

If we begin by considering plants, it's reasonable to deduce that a plant needs strong roots. Analogously, a human being needs courage in many of life's situations. However, expecting a human being to have courage is like saying,

*"…an owl should be able to see in the dark,"* or *"a gull should be able to recognize the sound of its chick among all the cacophony of the cliff."*

There is, says Foot, a *"gap between description of fact and evaluation."* The point is, if the man lacks courage, he is just as deprived as the owl with weak eyesight. The words Philippa Foot chooses to demonstrate the comparisons are important. Stating that the owl *should* have good eyesight, indicates how awkwardly that resonates with the idea that a human being *"should"* have courage. In either case, things are only what they are.

Further, what is necessary for optimum functioning of a living thing can be species-relevant. It's not necessary for human survival to have the ability to see in the dark, or detect the cries of our children amongst those of hundreds of others. But if an owl's eyes cannot function to see at night, then they are defective. If a gull cannot recognise a chick's cries; then, it too, is defective as a parent, according to its species.

*"These are the central notions,"* says Foot, *"And that's why I thought we should start moral philosophy by talking about plants."*

## Unquantified Propositions

The key to Foot's theory is an understanding of what she means by *"unquantified propositions."* She explains this to Rick Lewis:

*"This kind of proposition really is about the standard; it's about how it should be. It takes one towards what I have called 'natural goodness'. For example, we say 'humans have thirty two teeth.' Not all humans do, in fact, but we have defective teeth if we don't have thirty-two. Either we've never had the full complement or we've lost some."*

We cannot talk in this way about non-living things. A river cannot be defective. It just is what it is. It is subject to change, to seasons, but it cannot be talked about as defective. (It may be defective from our point of view, but not autonomously.)

## Different Ways of Understanding "Should"

So, we cannot talk about non-living things in the same way as we can talk about living things. She says, of non-living things, *"In the everyday use of language we do say 'it should' meaning 'it was about to' or 'they usually do' or something like that."*

She points out that a star being born is different from any member of a species being born. Rivers, as she states, don't actually flourish, and don't actually die in the sense that living creatures do.

*"They haven't got the pattern of one and then another of the same kind coming from it. Rivers don't spawn rivers… and there is in their case no species in which a function could be identified…"*

She continues, *"A spider's web has a function…to catch food…it will need in order to reproduce."*

References to non-living things are just statements of fact. They are about things without conscious awareness. Foot explains this important gap in semantics:

*"… that's not the same 'should'; that pattern doesn't give you the kind of natural defect. This is what I'm identifying here – the difference between the two."*

## Practical Rationality

*Should*, according to Foot, is about having reasons for our behaviour and actions, and she describes this as practical rationality, which embraces goodness in respect of beliefs and conclusions from premises. She tells Rick Lewis:

*"But then, you have to remember animals acting on instinct – and if they haven't got the right instincts, as a lioness who doesn't look after her cubs hasn't got the right instincts, then they are defective. Human beings work on instinct too, of course, but also they're taught to think."*

Foot does not accept that there is any necessity for reconciliation between morality and rationality, because, she says, they are not separate. In the first place, it is morality that takes a human being toward rationality, and not vice versa. We go for what we need, and we do this with prudence, which she claims is one of the virtues.

*"Why should it be thought that while prudence is certainly rational, morality isn't?"* she asks.

## The Pursuit of Happiness

Of course, for humans, part of rationality is the pursuit of happiness.

This brings Philippa Foot into uneven territory and she admits in the interview that she is left with a problem that seems impossible to solve. The problem is that humans don't flourish by merely achieving reproduction and a long life, characteristics that may be sufficient for a successful animal. (Other philosophers, Peter Singer for one, would disagree with Foot in this respect.) But it is true that human beings require happiness to flourish.

*"That's why I had to tackle the problem of happiness, and I found it extremely difficult. It's an articulated concept, it's very complex. I tried to describe it, to spread it out, but I was left with a really difficult problem which I couldn't solve… There is a really deep problem about the relation between virtue and happiness."*

*Can one describe a wicked person as a happy person? Of course one can."*

There are a great number of examples of how people have taken pleasure and gained happiness from terrible deeds, from cheating friends to torture and murder. Most human beings would feel ashamed of such actions, but there are those who glorify in abusive behaviour.

*"We cannot totally divorce the ideas of virtue and of happiness,"* concludes Foot.

Could you kill one person to save five?
Stonemason's yard. Photo by Janet Cameron,

## The Trolley Problem

Philippa Foot devised the famous moral paradox of *The Trolley Problem*. Here is a brief summary of the main points, presented by Josh Clark in his article *"How the Trolley Problem Works."*:

There is a runaway trolley on a railways track, heading straight for five people, who will be killed. You are near a lever, and you can pull it to divert the trolley and switching the trolley to a different track. But, on this other track. there is a man who will be killed if you take this action.

Would you pull the lever and sacrifice one to save five?

An alternative dilemma would be that there is a fat man, nearby, on a bridge. If you push him onto the track, his body will stop the train.

In both cases, pulling the lever, or pushing the fat man, will satisfy utilitarian principles, which require the greatest good for the greatest number, although you are involved in taking an action that causes loss of life.

Some people, who had no problem taking the utilitarian action in the first instance, were less willing to sacrifice the one man for the five, in the second example. As the author suggests, there seems to be a moral distinction between killing a person and taking no action and just letting a person die.

*"But philosophical questions like this have real-world implications for how people behave in society, governments, science, law and even war,"* says Josh Clark.

## Pioneer of Virtue Ethics

Philippa Foot was born on 3 October 1920 and died aged 90 on 23 October 2010. Although she worked at University of California beginning in 1976 for fifteen years, she maintained her close ties to Oxford all her life. Philippa Foot had a great influence in her capacity as a pioneer of virtue ethics. She had close links with other famous women philosophers at Oxford: Iris Murdoch, Elizabeth Anscombe and Mary Warnock.

Philippa Foot was a pioneer in virtue ethics, and posed one of the most challenging moral dilemmas in philosophical thought.

# Chapter 14

# Elizabeth Anscombe on Why Intentions Matter

Converting to Roman Catholicism inspired
Elizabeth Anscombe to theorise on morality.
Chichester Cathedral by Janet Cameron,

Gertrude Elizabeth Margaret Anscombe (1919-2001) was born in Limerick, Ireland. From 1970 to 1986, she was Professor of Philosophy at Cambridge.

Anscombe is also noted as being responsible for bringing Ludwig Wittgenstein to the public's attention; she met him during World War 2 at Cambridge, and attended his classes before becoming his greatest friend.

After Wittgenstein's death in 1951, Anscombe helped edit his posthumous material and translated his *Philosophical Investigations* to great acclaim. Neumann University describe her as

*"one of the twentieth century's most provocative and highly regarded philosophers."*

## Elizabeth Anscombe: The Rise of the Dragon Lady

This remarkable women, dubbed by some as *"The Dragon Lady"* and noted for her eccentricity, was enormously influential in moral philosophy. Elizabeth Anscombe was rude and unconventional; she liked to puff on a cigar, and, according to Jane O'Grady in her *Guardian* obituary,

*"Once, entering a smart restaurant in Boston, she was told that ladies were not admitted in trousers. She simply took them off."*

She caused an uproar in the establishment by saying exactly what she thought, however unpopular her views. Her views on sexual ethics were extremely conservative, and she upset the famous philosopher Bernard William by writing papers condemning both contraception and homosexuality.

Although Anscombe gave birth to seven children by her husband, philosopher Peter Geach, she always insisted being called *"Miss Anscombe"* – a stance that caused raised eyebrows in polite society.

Anscombe was devoutly Roman Catholic, and it was her religious conversion that inspired her passion for the nature of morality and virtue ethics. Her other main interest was the meaning and limits of language.

*"Bluff, courageous, determined, loyal, she argued that the word 'I' does not refer to anything, but she certainly believed in the soul,"* says Jane O'Grady.

## Anscombe's Theory of Right and Wrong

In *Elizabeth Anscombe,* Jane O'Grady explains how Anscombe's philosophical theory was more

*"systematic and thoroughgoing than Wittgenstein's cryptic suggestive hints, and was also, distinctively, her own."*

Anscombe argues that moral obligations, duties, rights and wrongs are out of date, and originate from the Judeo-Christian law of God. While she believes in God, she criticises the way we use language. For Anscombe, it is not the case that *"the right action is the one that produces the best possible consequences."*

## Anti-Deterministic Theory of Intentions

Elizabeth Anscombe was fiercely anti-deterministic, and this is integral to her work in the nature of intentionality. If determinism is valid, then we are not free to act as we choose. Therefore, it is senseless to assign responsibility to people for their actions. If we believe in determinism, then only consequences can matter.

We are subject to both intentional rational behaviour and non-rational behaviour. If we have a twitch, or any other involuntary action, although this behaviour might have a cause, it is certainly not one of intention. There would be no reason for us, intentionally, to move in this way.

Intentional action is different. It's about the meaning of actions. We can ask another person to tell us the reason behind their action, or their purpose in deciding to behave in that way.

*"This sets them* [intentional actions] *apart from questions about causes, since I might not know what caused me to sleep so restlessly but I cannot be so ignorant of my intentions. I could hypothesize that dehydration caused me to sleep badly, but if I*

get up to drink some water then it is no hypothesis on my part that I am heading to the kitchen to get something to drink." (Quoted from the *Internet Encyclopedia of Philosophy [IEP].)*

Consequentialism, a term she invented, is suspect because it justifies execution of an innocent person as a possibly correct action. Anscombe sees this as corrupt.

*"For men to choose to kill the innocent as a means to their ends is always murder,"* she says, adhering to Aristotle's concepts of virtue and reason. This statement resonates with a confrontation with her university over the bombing of Hiroshima and Nagasaki, which she considered mass murder.

In *"Professor G.E.M. Anscombe,"* the *Telegraph*'s obituary reporter says:

*"… in 1956, she caused something of a sensation when she opposed the conferment of an honorary degree by Oxford on President Truman. In her essay, 'Mr Truman's Degree,' she pointed out that he had been responsible for the bombing of Hiroshima and Nagasaki, and that the consequent death of innocents, even as a necessary means to an end, remained murder. 'You may not do evil,' ran her injunction, 'that good may come.'"*

## All Modern Philosophers are Consequentialists

Anscombe applies the moral theory of consequentialism, which she opposes, to all modern moral philosophers beginning with Henry Sidgwick (1838-1900.) She raises these issues in her most important work, *Modern Moral Philosophy.*

*The Internet Encyclopedia of Philosophy's* article *"Elizabeth Anscombe (1919-2001)"* says:

*"Contemporary interest in virtue theory can be traced directly to this paper, which put forward three theses: that all the major British moral philosophers from Henry Sidgwick on were essentially the same (that is, consequentialists); that the concepts of moral obligation, the use of the word "ought" with a special moral sense, and related notions, are harmful and should be dropped; and that we should stop doing moral philosophy until we have an adequate philosophy of psychology."*

Here is another more dramatic example from the *IEP* article, describing the necessity of defining intentionality:

*"To see this point more clearly, imagine a climber who loses the will to live and so lets go of the rock and falls to his death. This was intentional, an act of suicide. Now imagine that he simply loses his grip and falls. This is unintentional and not suicide but a tragic accident."*

## The Importance of Establishing Intention

Generally, unintentional behaviour is not something we would be judgmental about since it would be irrelevant to ethics, but intentional behaviour is what ethics is all about. For example, regarding the example in the previous paragraph, many religious people consider suicide a mortal sin.

Generally, we know very well what our intentions are, and it is vital to understand the difference between intentional, rational behaviour, and non-rational behaviour. However, sometimes our intentions don't play out quite as we have planned. The following quotation from the *IEP* article, explains how human error and mistakes can thwart intentions.

*"It is possible to act badly because of having a bad intention, of course, but it is also possible… for action to go wrong because of errors in execution."* (The example given is the intention of writing a name on a chalkboard, but the board is slippery and the chalk makes no mark.)

## Anscombe's Works

Besides her *Modern Moral Philosophy,* there are three-volumes of *Collected Philosophical Papers* (1981), which covers epistemology, metaphysics, history of philosophy, and philosophy of religion.

*Causality and Determination* is her inaugural lecture on becoming professor of Cambridge in 1970. Other papers, quoted by Neumann University and included in their March 2014 conference, are *Catholic Moral Theory, Double Effect, Souls and Persons,* and *Marriage and Women.*

# CHAPTER 15

# Dame Iris Murdoch (1919-1999): "Can We Be Good Without God?"

Murdoch says we can have religion and morality
without God – as the Buddhists do.
Photo by Janet Cameron, all Rights Reserved.

Must humans move on from their mythical childhood? Should we– or can we– change religion into philosophy? Would this become a threat to our religious culture?

In *Metaphysics as a Guide to Morals,* Iris Murdoch suggests that in these times of change, it might be prudent to discard the old word *"God"* as it suggests an omniscient spectator and a responsive *"Superthou."*

She continues by asserting the obvious truth that religion can and does exist without the Western concept of a personal God. It certainly achieves this already, in the religions of Buddhism and Hinduism.

As Murdoch explains:

*"…religion involving supernatural belief (as in a literal after-life) was always partly a kind of illusion… we are now being forced by an inevitable sophistication to have a demythologised religion or none at all."*

## Changing Religion into Philosophy

Murdoch describes the ways in which Protestants and Catholics view each other's rituals and procedures with dismay. Instead, she argues for

*"…a moral philosophy which accommodates the unconditional element in the structure of reason and reality."*

Murdoch wants moral philosophy to include political philosophy and the morality of political thinking and she believes that art and philosophy *"enliven the concept of reality."*

In defining her stance, she says: *"Nothing is more important for theology and philosophy than the truth it contains."*

## The Connection between the Good and the Moral

Murdoch falls back on Plato, whose influence has always been part of her philosophical thought. She says:

*"Plato's philosophy expounds a fundamental connection between epistemology and ethics; truthful knowledge and virtue are bound together."*

For Iris Murdoch, as for Plato himself, thought, truth and reality are inescapably linked.

Murdoch explains that, according to Plato, good is something distant, ideal and abstract; but it is not the function of, or the outcome of, desire or human will. Human beings are naturally drawn to good merely by apprehending it. The degree to which we are attracted by the good depends on our own personal morality– we need to be virtuous in order to apprehend it.

Murdoch also recognises the bind we are in, and our reluctance to lose elements of our culture should we move away from theology and metaphysics in order to embrace scientific thought.

So what will happen to human morality if religion is demythologised? What will happen to our concept of God?

## The Ontological Proof is Limited

In her Chapter, "*The Ontological Proof*" in *Metaphysics as a Guide to Morals,* Murdoch examines aspects of the various proofs of God's existence. Some proofs rely on early concepts, such as cosmic design, or a first cause. Murdoch is swift to dispense with these, for now we have more substantial ways of accounting for the cosmos through science and technology.

With regard to cosmic design, she says the argument is unsound in any case:

*"Why should swallows have to fly to Africa every year?"* and *"Why should we venerate a Supreme Being, whose most convincing claim to existence is that of having created an impressive machine? A demon could have created the world."*

Murdoch quotes Arthur Schopenhauer, who called the ontological proof *"a charming joke."* She is positive that God does not, and cannot, exist, and examines a number of further *"proofs"* to confirm her position.

## Fatal Flaws in the Ontological Argument

St. Anselm of Canterbury, who lived from 1033-1109, produced several hypotheses, one of which was that the *idea* of God exists, therefore, God must exist.

St. Anselm had conceived of the existence of God in his imagination, and he claimed it is much greater to exist in reality than merely in the Imagination. He *"reasoned"* therefore, that there must be a supreme, perfect being.

Immanuel Kant, in the 18th century, demolished Anselm's theory and pointed out that his proof was fatally flawed, since existence did not presuppose perfection. In her book, Murdoch discounts several other religious proofs.

## The Meaning of God

Murdoch attempts to address the definition of the concept of God:

*"I think that the confusion arises from attempts to extend the meaning of our word, God, to cover any conception of a spiritual reality. This move, which saves the concept through a sort of liberal vagueness, clouds over the problem without solving it. 'God' is the name of a supernatural person. It makes a difference whether we believe in such a person, as it makes a difference whether we believe that Christ rose from the dead."*

However, Murdoch believes that these differences do not actually have any effect on whether or not we are virtuous, although she accepts that relinquishing religious belief may have negative effects on moral thought and action, provided for by church and prayer.

Contemplation of a work of art is a spiritual experience.
Photo by Janet Cameron, all Rights Reserved.

## The Spiritual in Art and Beauty

In his article, *"Murdoch, an unlikely liberal icon,"* in *The Guardian*, Hywel Williams says:

*"Murdoch said she hated the ego in all its selfish, sentimental mess and its craving for dominion. Art– especially romantic art– fed the self. But, being human, Murdoch was inconsistent. Her divide between art and philosophy was always breaking down."*

The problem seems to stem from her failure to reconcile her love of life and entertainment, as embodied in her novels, and her conviction of the need to *"unself"* in her philosophy.

However, in *Experiment in the Modern Novel,* John Carrington indicates that Murdoch seems not to regard this as a difficulty:

*"'Happiness,' Iris Murdoch wrote, 'is being busy and lively and unconcerned with self… to be damned is for one's ordinary, everyday mode of consciousness to be unremitting, agonising, preoccupation with self.'"*

Clearly, being unconscious of self does not necessarily equate with being miserable and deprived.

Murdoch says the best kind of thinking is perception, and the best of all is contemplative perception, when we look upon something beautiful, a flower, a work of art, or listen to music. This, she says, is *"presence."* She quotes from Simone Weil's Notebooks:

*"Ontological proof is mysterious because it does not address itself to the intelligence, but to love."*

## The Good is *"Above Being"*

The definition of God, says Murdoch, is related to the definition of a human being. *"We can think away material objects from human existence, but not the concepts of good, true and real."*

She then asks why the concept of certainty should resonate with such importance.

*"It adheres essentially to the conception of being human, and cannot be detached; and we may express this by saying that it is not accidental, does not exist contingently, is above being."*

Murdoch, does, in the end, embrace the concept of the good as spiritual, as suggested by experience. She claims it is:

*"… true enough to exhibit as fundamental, our sense of the purely good as, essentially, beyond us… the truth, the light… [it] floats free from contingent detail and is not at the mercy of history…*It is something *"central and mysterious and most real."*

# Iris Murdoch's Life and Work

Iris Murdoch was born in Dublin of Anglo-Irish parents, and went on lecture at Oxford, and later at the Royal College of Arts, in philosophy. Her literary output was impressive, and her entry in *Literature in English* says, of her novels: *"With their blend of realism and symbolism, they reflect her interest in psychological patterns and myths in human relationships. Their narrative skill and talent for irony has also helped attract a wide readership. "*

Murdoch explained that…

*"…the energy of philosophical problem"* drove her plots. As Carrington summarises: *"an unusual mix of psychological realism, poetic symbolism, mystery and humour."*

# CHAPTER 16

# Mary Warnock: The Ethics of Cloning as an Acceptable Infertility Treatment

Ethics philosophers debate the morality of extending
cloning from sheep to people. Image by hotlack

Is cloning acceptable? It depends on your philosophy.

Ethics philosopher, Baroness Mary Warnock, addressed the dilemma over whether
cloning could ever become a morally acceptable treatment for infertility.

Warnock's ethics philosophy concluded that cloning should be off-limits until it is
proven safe and risk-free, while others have embraced the idea of duplicating
humans, regardless of potential complications.

## Baroness Mary Warnock: Ethics Philosopher

Warnock, born in 1924 in Winchester, England, has a distinguished career behind her, as she champions philosophical issues related to human rights, morality and education. Her specialty, ethics, examines issues of human values, how we live, how we decide between right and wrong and similar moral concepts. She has also written extensively on existentialism, a relatively modern philosophy which holds that all people have freedom of choice and are responsible for their own lives.

## What is Important About Ethics Philosophy?

Ethics and morality change the way we view the world. What one person regards as their "right" might grievously offend another person on purely moral grounds. From a public perspective this "right" might be seen as unjust, as in the case of the right of a woman to have an abortion as opposed to the right of the human foetus to be protected for its own sake.

Warnock points out:

*"Rights are part of the structure of a society; in nature there are neither rights nor duties."*

She makes an important distinction between legal and moral rights. Legal rights are those supported by law, such as the right to 'free speech' in the United States Constitution, whereas moral rights *"belong to all humans in view of their humanity."* Moral rights are not necessarily related to law. Instead, they would find their roots in principles and a sense of moral obligation. Warnock admits this can be a difficult distinction.

# The Morality of Human Cloning

Mary Warnock addresses whether the cloning of humans would be intrinsically wrong. She acknowledges that, though human reproductive cloning may not be possible within the foreseeable future, it would be wrong to subject fellow humans to such risk and uncertainty. According to Warnock, even if there are willing participants, scientists should not, in their pursuit of such a radical procedure, exploit people's desperation for children.

However, assuming the risks involved have been eliminated, is human cloning still morally unacceptable? After all, identical twins sharing identical DNA are common; they don't cause moral outrage. So what is it about the human clone that makes us edgy?

It's not relevant, for example, to claim that a clone would be born without a proper human identity. "*Even Siamese twins are commonly held to have distinct identities,*" as Warnock says.

Another objection is that it would be tough for a cloned child to see a parent age. Watching this aging, the child would know "know" the outcome of his or her own life. Warnock dismisses this with some disdain.

"*There are already numerous sons who inherit genes from their father… such as a tendency to early baldness.*"

# Cloning: The Slippery Slope

The Slippery Slope theory is the belief that if "X" happens, then "Y" and "Z" will automatically follow. "X" is fairly harmless – we can live with it. However, if "X" leads to "Y" which is more challenging, then "Z" will follow. "Z" is the most undesirable outcome.

World-famous Dolly the cloned sheep was born in 1997. Sadly, for Dolly, the cloning process didn't result in good health; she died at only six years old, prematurely aged and suffering from arthritis.

According to NBC News, Canadian dentist, Michael Zuk, has purchased and preserved one of John Lennon's teeth. Allegedly, Zuk has begun the process of sequencing, hoping to transform the Beatle's DNA from tissue to stem cells. Zuk firmly believes he will eventually present the world with a clone of the famous Beatle.

Is it right to create a person with the same technology that resulted in Dolly's unfortunate end?  Warnock points out:

*"Producing a human clone seems to be the ultimate and most extreme example of the manipulation of human beings. It is not that each individual clone child would be deprived of free will; he would be as much free and as much determined as the rest of us… The fear is rather that some person, or some regime, might one day exercise such power that people could be born to their command, in the numbers they dictated, and, worst of all, with the characteristics they thought desirable."*

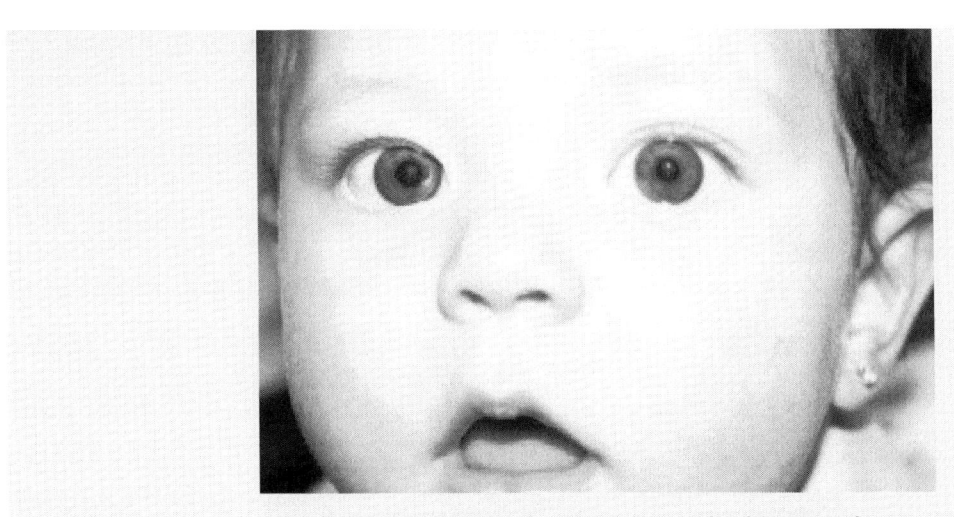

Should there be laws against cloning people
to create the perfect baby? Image by octaviolopez

# Designer Babies and Parental Vanity: Morally Wrong?

The idea brings to mind Aldous Huxley's *A Brave New World,* and current arguments about designer babies, born to satisfy the vanity of the parents. Does it feel morally wrong that we should have this kind of power over another human being? As always, it depends on your personal philosophy.

Wesley J. Smith says, in his article, <u>The Time Has Come to Outlaw Human Cloning</u>,

*"It is the ultimate in desensitization… the problem, one could almost say, is not what cloning does to the embryo, but what it does to us… If everything is permitted then there are no fences, no safeguards, no bottom."*

Many people find the idea morally abhorrent, and Mary Warnock herself welcomes the *"efficient methods of licensing and control that we have in the UK."*

# CHAPTER 17

# Part 1: Philosopher Mary Midgley: Are You an Illusion?

Life was there from Our Beginnings.

Philosophy, as a discipline, is vulnerable to fashion as much as any other. At least, so says Andrew Anthony, in his interview, *"Late Stand for a Thinker with Soul"* for *The Observer*.

His subject is 94 year-old moral philosopher, Mary Midgley, who has just published a book entitled, *Are You an Illusion?*

This is the old, old argument. Are we, as human beings, the sum total of our physical properties, as is the viewpoint of the materialists, for example, Richard Dawkins? Or are we much more than that?  Mary Midgley thinks so. For Midgley, human consciousness equates with *soul.*

Andrew Anthony recognises the dilemma.  He says:

*"And currently there is what might be called a battle for the human soul being fought between the humanities and the sciences over who is best placed to examine the nature of consciousness and what it means to be human."*

## Mary Midgley's Character

It seems that the topic of the self is rising in popularity, and with it, so are the views of Mary Midgley. Anthony acknowledges the forbidding nature of Midgley's character, juxtaposed with an underlying and endearing, *"mischievous sense of humour."*

This brings to mind comments in Andrew Brown's 2001 *Guardian Unlimited* article:

*"…our foremost scourge of scientific pretension… staunch defender of religion…although she doesn't believe in God… may be the most frightening philosopher in the country: the one before whom it is least pleasant to appear a fool."*

## Midgley's Arch Enemy – Richard Dawkins

Midgley dismisses Dawkins' views as "scientism" and attacked him vociferously after the publication of his book *The Selfish Gene*, in spite of general acclaim.

*"Everyone was telling him he was the cat's whiskers, you see, and I wasn't."*

Anthony describes Midgley's stance against Dawkins,

*"…a kind of self-defeating fatalism, namely the conviction that the universe has no purpose, that it contains, at bottom, as Dawkins has written, nothing but blind, pitiless indifference."*

Dawkins, of course, is uncompromisingly an atheist. In response to a Canadian critic quoted in his book *The God Delusion*, when asked if the world would be a more humane place if people looked to *The God Delusion* instead of *The Bible* for truth and comfort, Dawkins responds that he does feel it would be more humane, because *"consolation-content of a belief does not raise its truth-value."* In this belief, Dawkins is unwavering.

## Our Universe Demonstrates Purpose

Mary Midgley, however, seems not to be inflexible, and acknowledges that there is much we cannot know for certain. However, according to her, there is evidence that there is purpose to our lives. She sees purpose in the very act of life, and in the acts of each and every organism, reaching out to fulfil their potential, each kind in its own specific way.

For Midgley, there is not necessarily a God, but she likes to talk about the *"life-force"* and its move towards complexity. Whatever this is, in her view it is not DNA or some scientific theory, but *"something that gives rise to them."*

Through Andrew Anthony, Midgley quotes her philosophical ally, Thomas Nagel, who reportedly said,

*"…the possibility of the development of conscious organisms must have been built into the world from the beginning. It cannot be an accident."*

However, this is not a way of describing life as coming about through *"intelligent design."* The concept of intelligent design came into being through people misconstruing the work of Charles Darwin.

Mary Midgley wrote *"The Solitary Self, Darwin and the Selfish Gene,"* in 2010 in order to combat Dawkins' arguments; she claims she did this out of "exasperation."

Every Organism Has a Life Force.
Image copyright Janet Cameron, all rights reserved.

## Midgley's Argument with Francis Crick, Co-Disoverer of DNA

Midgley's latest work, *Are You an Illusion,* targets Francis Crick, who co-discovered DNA. In the book, she quotes Crick:

*"You, your joys and your sorrows, your memories and your ambitions, your sense of personal identity and free will, are in fact, no more than the behaviour of a vast assembly of nerve cells and their attendant molecules."*

Midgley strongly refutes the possibility that our *"self"* could possibly be the result of an elaborate trick played upon us by our nerve cells and she scorns what she describes as "dogmatic materialism."

## Women Philosophers

Anthony briefly cites Midgley's time at Oxford during World War II, when she was part of a group of female philosophers including Philippa Foot, Iris Murdoch, Elizabeth Anscombe and Mary Warnock. All of these went on to work in moral philosophy and/or ethics.

At this time, Midgley wrote to *The Guardian*, says Anthony, explaining that men had done *"good enough philosophy in the past,"* but that their method was competition in argument.

*"These people then quickly build up a set of games out of simple oppositions and elaborate them, until, in the end, nobody else can see what they are talking about."*

Indeed, a fellow philosopher, John Ree, said of her:

*"She has always written in a language that's not aimed at the cleverest graduate student. She's never been interested in the glamour and greasy pole."*

## Life Goes Back to the Origins of the Universe

Andrew Anthony challenged Midgley for her stance in attempting to make sense of an *"indifferent universe."* She simply asked if he wanted some sort of proof,

*"…as if there was some kind of proof that wouldn't go through oneself. There can't be, can there?"*

Instead, she feels that from the Big Bang onwards, there has been a move towards order, and this has produced life, and then it has produced perceptive life. She simply refuses to take on board that this is superstition. *"It's still very vague, of course."* All the same, she feels that our tendency to search for order draws us towards meaning. Importantly, the life force also draws us towards righteousness and the desire to make things better.

Our beginnings were not simple. Our consciousness is natural.

# Philosophy is Like Plumbing

Mary Midgley has a charming analogy for philosophy. She compares it to plumbing. You don't notice it until things go wrong.

# Mary Midgley

# Part 2: Should We Seek Biological Immortality?

Adam and Eve are Condemned to Mortality.

Danse Macabre, Hans Holbein, Image by McLeod.

Can the human race achieve biological immortality, so that we can live forever? This may sound delusional, but there *are* certain organisms that appear to live forever, at least, in theory. Philosopher Mary Midgley questions whether we should seek biological immortality, if it becomes scientifically possible.

## Works by Mary Midgley

Mary Midgley, a lecturer at the University of Newcastle-upon-Tyne, retired in 1980. Her works include *Beast and Man* (1978); *Animals and Why They Matter* (1983) and *Evolution as a Religion* (1985.) She received *Philosophy Now*'s 2011 Award for *Contributions in the Fight Against Stupidity.*

## Immortality – Possibility or Delusion?

If physical immortality is possible for human beings, do we want it? Or, maybe more to the point, *should* we want it?

In her article, *"Death and the Human Animal"* in *Philosophy Now*, Mary Midgley voices some strong objections to the new immortalist movement's claims.

Campaigner, Aubrey de Grey, says *"Humans have a right to live as long as they wish."* The immortalists believe that this will soon be possible and that we will, eventually, become immortal.

Midgley, a moral and animal rights philosopher, firmly ascribes this to

*"…the kind of individualism that is now in fashion, combined with a devout faith in medical technology which was not present in past ages."*

Midgley asks, rather disdainfully, whether egos are being deified, but acknowledges:

*"There is actually more room for debate here than one might expect because the reasons for aging and death have always been obscure. There is some reason to think that no specially-wired mechanism to produce death and aging exists because it has never been needed."*

Midgley questions the demographics, asking who gets immortality first. For example, if the rich and influential are first in line, would advances set up a new inequality?

# Population Control in an Immortal Society

Mary Midgley believes that our resources are not infinite and that space cannot be stretched. If we achieved immortality, we would have to stop having children altogether.

*"This would be a pretty dramatic change. Is it actually a change for the better?"* she asks, *"No doubt children are annoying, but people still seem fairly sure they want to have them… And how would it be if no new people ever arrived in society?"*

Midgley also asks about the other end of life, old age, when we would need to decide what would be the proper age for pensions.

The influx of a number of revived bodies does not, explains Midgley, concern the *"high priest of cryonics"* as she describes Robert Ettinger. Midgley cites Bryan Appleyard's book *How to Live Forever or Die Trying:"* in which he quotes Ettinger:

*"The frozen population would increase by four billion every thirty years. If it takes 300 years for civilization to reach the immortality level, there would then be some forty billion people to revive and relocate – if we assume, for simplicity, that it all happens at once… There is ample room on our planet for forty billion people.*

Mary Midgley questioned the wisdom
of attempting biological immortality.
Image by MPMWikihelper.

Christine Gaspar, in her article, *"Can Transhumanism and the Everyman Co-Exist"* claims overpopulation would be unlikely, since the more educated people became, the fewer children they were likely to have. Gaspar, a registered nurse and President of the Cryonics Society of Canada, does not explain, in the article, how we could be certain such an outcome could be achieved. (Transhumanism is the philosophy of improving the human condition through knowledge and technology and Gaspar claims that "cryonics" is a part of it.)

Midgley evaluates the attitude of De Grey and other immortalists as being too narrow and personal, a stance taken by those unwilling to accept their mortality at the expense of the broader picture. According to Midgley, they do not concern themselves with overpopulation and inequality:

*"these are evils which already invade us today and which can't possibly be kept separate from problems about an increased lifespan."*

## Alone in a Far-Flung Future

Christine Gaspar raises the question of coming back, maybe decades or centuries from now, without any of the people who were dear to us. She has dealt with this fear by persuading her family and friends to sign up themselves to the cryonics project as well.

However, Mary Midgley is convinced that a life that was eternal would be boring, unlivable and repetitive. She asks about…

*"…the inborn emotional constitution that guides us through life. Can that constitution expand its scope indefinitely so as (for instance) to go far beyond great grandchildren – to take in an indefinite succession of descendants? Or, alternatively, if all childbearing stops and there are no new people, can it go on finding enough to occupy it by interacting with the circle of friends already here?"*

## Physical Immortality in Nature

Setting aside hypotheticals, there are bizarre cases where it appears that living creatures can go on forever naturally. These include, for example, the amoeba, which reproduces by continually dividing. There is also the strange case of the tiny immortal jellyfish that has now colonised most of our temperate and tropical oceans, and is able to reverse its life cycle.

Recently, however, David Attenborough told the *Radio Times* that human beings may have stopped evolving because of birth control – so maybe it's a step too far to imagine we can reverse our life cycles like the jellyfish.

## If We Were Codfish…

Mortality is the price we pay for our complexity, our individuality, our inquisitiveness and our humanity. *"We are not pure minds or abstract energies,"* says Midgley. *"We are mammals."*

The reality is that we experience love of companionship, demonstrate parenting skills and display inquisitiveness. These characteristics make us what we are.

*"If we were codfish, none of these things would be true,"* says Midgley.

# CHAPTER 18

# Mary Beard on the Silencing of Women's Voices

Mary Beard speaks to women about
being heard and respected.

In her lecture, *"Oh Do Shut Up, Dear,"* Professor Mary Beard quoted a typical modern-day male technique that silences women in the boardroom. She calls it *"The Failed Intervention."*

The woman takes her turn to speak, then waits, expecting a response relevant to her argument. Then a man will intercede, picking up from a previous comment: *"What I was saying was…"* he begins again, with no reference to what she has just said.

It is as though she does not exist; as though nothing of any consequence has happened during the previous few moments. The men ignore her, dehumanize her–and silence her!

People usually instruct women in this position to disregard the insult and *"keep mum."*

*"An integral part of growing up as a man is learning to take control of public utterance and to silence the female of the species,"* says Mary Beard.

This has happened throughout history. The fact that it still happens today is a matter for serious concern. Professor Mary Beard of Cambridge University, a charismatic and accomplished speaker, delivered her lecture in the British Museum to a captive audience.

## The Ancient Art of Silencing Women, from Life and Literature

There are numerous examples in literature of female characters being routinely silenced.  These are just a few, quoted by Beard, in her lecture:

In Homer's *The Odyssey*, written around three thousand years ago, Telemachus tells his mother Penelope: *"Go back to your quarters… Speech will be the business of men, all men, and of me most of all, for mine is the power in the household."*

Much later, in the early 4th Century BC, Aristophanes wrote a comedy fantasy about women taking over the running of the state. The men thought it was hilarious, since women were *"unable to speak properly in public."*

In Ovid's *Metamorphoses,* Zeus turns one female character, Io, into a cow and she can only "moo." Zeus' wife, Hera, punishes another, Echo, by not allowing her control over her own voice. She can only repeat the words of others.

One of the main techniques used to silence women has frequently been that of scorn and derision. Men accused assertive women of those times of being androgynous and freakish; in other words, a female form with a man's nature. They described female speech as *"yapping"* or *"barking."*

A lecturer and guru, Dio Chrysostom from the second century, posited a situation where *"an entire community experienced a strange affliction. The men's voices became female. No one could speak in a manly manner."* The learned "guru" concluded it would be worse than the plague.

## The Art of Silencing Women in Life and on Social Networks

The intention to silence is still practised in modern life, although different methods may be used, for example, that of abuse or attack through social media. Recently, the support for a female logo on a banknote evoked outrage and abusive comments on *Twitter.*

Distressingly, someone who disliked Beard's politics sent her sick, abusive tweets. When she objected, tweeting that she was *"gobsmacked,"* one male commentator responded, *"'The misogyny is truly gobsmacking,' she whined."* The same commentator quoted above runs a "lighthearted" sideline. This is a contest to find *"...the most stupid woman to appear on Question Time."*

Through social media, Beard has also been called an *"ignorant moron"* and she has been threatened with sickening physical violence.

Women receive threatening (including death threats) and sexually abusive tweets more frequently than men, with thirty women targeted for every single male, says Beard. Further, although women who speak in public today are not normally described as *"barking"* or *"yapping,"* critics often call them *"strident."*

From these few, brief examples we can see how prejudice against women speaking in public is still with us. While Beard agrees that Western culture cannot entirely place the blame on the Greeks and Romans for our present-day gendered speaking, their culture, rules and conventions remain with us.

*"The modern techniques of rhetoric and persuasion formulated in the Renaissance were drawn explicitly from ancient speeches and handbooks,"* she says.

Authority figures from the nineteenth century were taught in this way, and today we still experience this subversive influence.

Mary Beardsley Lecturing in the British Museum.
Image by Janet Cameron, all rights reserved.

## Margaret Thatcher's Voice Training

The tradition of gendered speaking goes right back into ancient history, to Aristotle and to Cicero. According to Mary Beard, President Obama uses rhetorical "tricks" taken directly from Cicero.

When Britain elected Margaret Thatcher Prime Minister, advisors considered it necessary to raise her profile – by lowering the pitch of her voice. As it was, it simply was not "authoritative" enough.

*"And that's fine, in a way, if it works,"* says Mary Beard, *"but all tactics of that type tend to leave women still feeling on the outside, impersonators of rhetorical roles that they don't feel they own.*

*"Putting it bluntly, having women pretend to be men may be a quick fix, but it doesn't get to the heart of the problem."*

Beard says there is no reason within our culture that we should perceive a male voice as exuding more authority. Nor is there any neurological reason why this should be so.

Why, then, do we accept that the deep timbre of a male voice has a superior and more authoritative quality except that tradition drums this into us, and has become hard-wired into our brains?

## Consciousness-Raising Tactics

The truth is, as Mary Beard explains, that women pay a very high price in order to be heard. She points out that the public regards men with craggy, wrinkled faces as mature and wise, where the same people consider women of a similar age and cragginess as *"past their use-by date."* She concludes her lecture with the following suggestion:

*"What we need is some old fashioned consciousness-raising about what we mean by the voice of authority and how we've come to construct it. We need to work that out before we figure out how we modern Penelopes might answer back to our own Telemachuses."*

# Conclusion

As we have seen, women have shown considerable expertise, especially in the "applied" fields of morality and ethics. Their work has had impact on politics and how we endeavor to live the best lives we can today. At the same time, great work has been achieved in applying metaphysics to issues of morality and ethics.

However, we should not forget the great achievements and sacrifices made by those women mavericks who bucked the system before the label of "feminism" was coined.

Of course, these wonderful women are only a selection from a small part of the history of women who risked everything.  There are others who are equally deserving of recognition, and, no doubt, modern women will investigate and discover much more that has been long-hidden.

Women's philosophy has a long and complex history just waiting to be revealed

And that's important.

# Bibliography:

Socrates Scholasticus. *The Life of Hypatia.* (305-445 AD). Ecclesiastical History. Accessed October 13, 2013.

Rich, Adrienne. *Diving into the Wreck: The Fact of a Doorframe.* (1984). W.W. Norton and Company.

The Economist. *The Tale of Marasaki Shikibu.* (December 1990). Accessed on September 13, 2015

Foreman, Amanda. *The Ascent of Women Part 2.* (2015). BBC. Acacessed on September 13, 2015

Shikibu, Murasaki. *The Tale of Genji (Review).* Goodreads. Accessed on September 13, 2015

Conley, John J. *Marie le Jars de Gournay.* Internet Encyclopedia of Philosophy. Accessed on May 02, 2014

Auffret, Séverine. *Marie de Gournay, Marie de Gournay du Les temerities d'une quenoillle.* Accessed on May 02, 2014

Women-philosophers.com. *Marie le Jars de Gournay..* Accessed on May 02, 2014

University of Chicago Press. *To the Queen 1 on presenting her with the Equality of Men and Women..*Wollstonecraft, Mary. (1792). Columbia University. Accessed October 7, 2013.

Matthews, Susan. *Women Writers and Readers, Romantic Writings.* (1996). Routledge in association with The Open University.

McIlroy, W.J. *Without the Faith.* (2007). Brighton and Hove Humanist Society.

Calder, Angus, et al. *Literature and Gender.* (1996). Routledge with The Open University.

Bio. A&E TV Networks. *Sojourner Truth: Biography.* Accessed on October 26, 2014

Lennon, Kathleen. *Feminine Perspectives on the Body.* (2014). Stanford Encyclopedia of Philosophy. Accessed on October 26, 2014

Rose, Ernestine. A *Lecture on Women's Rights 1851.*
http://womhist.alexanderstreet.com. Accessed on April 21, 2014

Brandeis University. About Ernestine Rose. Accessed on April 21, 2014

MacFarlane, Alistair. *Ada Lovelace...on how a poet's daughter invented the concept of software.* (2013). Anja Publications Ltd..

San Diego Supercomputer Center. *Ada Byron, Countess of Lovelace.* (1997). Accessed on January 12, 2014

*Finding Ada.* (Accessed 10 January 2014). Accessed on January 12, 2014

Hooper, Rowan, et al. Ada Lovelace: *My brain is more than merely mortal.* (Accessed 10 January 2014). New Scientist. Accessed on January 12, 2014

agnesscot.edu. Ada, The Enchantress of Numbers.. (Accessed 10 January 2014). Accessed on January 12, 2014

Babbage, Charles, et al. *Sketch of the Analytical Engine Invented by Charles Babbage with Notes by the Translator Ava Lovelace.* (Accessed 10 January 2014). Accessed on January 12, 2014

Moon, Amy, et al. Ada, *The Enchantress of Numbers.* (20 April, 1998, Accessed 10 January 2014). Accessed on January 12, 2014

Dr. Betty , Toole, et al. *Ada Byron, Lady Lovelace.* (Accessed 10 January 2014). Strawberry Press. Accessed on January 12, 2014.

Schiavone, Louise. *Even in stone suffragettes cause a stir on Capitol Hill.* (1997). Washington CNN. Accessed on October 22, 2014

Halsall, Paul. *The Declaration of Sentiments, Seneca Falls, 1848*. (1997). Fordham University. Accessed on October 22, 2014

Goodman, Lizbeth. *Literature and Gender.* (1996). Routledge and The Open University.

bio. A & E TV Networks, LLC. *Elizabeth Cady Stanton*. (2014). Accessed on October 22, 2014.

Exploring Constitutional Conflicts. *Women's Fight for the Vote*. Accessed on October 22, 2014

O'Neill, Patrick. *Ayn Rand and the Is/Ought Problem.* (Spring 1983). The State University of New York, Binghampton. Accessed on February 25, 2014
Murdoch, Iris. *Metaphysics as a Guide to Morals.* (1993). Penguin Books.

Russell, Bertrand. *David Hume, History of Western Philosophy.* (2004). Routledge Classics.

Rand, Ayn. *The Virtue of Selfishness.* (1964). New American Library.

Harwood, Jeremy. *Ayn Rand, Philosophy, 100 Great Thinkers.* (2010). Quercus.

Butler, Judith. Hannah Arendt's challenge to Adolf Eichmann. (2011). The Guardian. Accessed December 3, 2013.

Katz, Pamela. *Hannah Arendt.* (2012). Margarethe von Trotta; Director. Duke of York PIcturehouse, Brighton, UK. Accessed November 27, 2013.

Rosenberg, Laurence. Exploring the Holocaust through Hannah Arendt's "Banality of Evil." (2009). *The Jewish Magazine.*

Harwood, Jeremy. *"Hannah Arendt."* (2010). Philosophy. 100 Great Thinkers. Quercus.

Beauvoir, de, Simone. *The Second Sex.* (1949,1953). Jonathan Cape.

Walter, Natasha. *"Let Boys Wear Pink,"The New Feminism.* (1998). Little, Brown and Company.

Wollstonecraft, Mary. *A Vindication of the Rights of Women.* (1792 – 1992). Everyman.

Harwood, Jeremy. *100 Great Thinkers.* (2010). Quercus,

Bergoffen, Debra. *Stanford Encyclopedia of Philosophy.* (2010). Metaphysics Research Lab, CSLI, Stanford University. Accessed November 18, 2013.

Bragg, Melvyn, et al. *In Our Time.* (2012). BBC Radio 4. Accessed on May 11, 2014

Murdoch, Iris. *Metaphysics as a Guide to Morals.* (1992). Penguin Books.

Goodwin, Gary. *Mystical Experiences of Simone Weil.* Mystical Experience Registry. Accessed on May 11, 2014

Harwood, Jeremy. *Philosophy, 100 Great Thinkers.* (2010). Quercus.

Weil, Simone. *Gravity and Grace.* (2002). Routledge Classics.

Weil, Simone. *The Need for Roots: Prelude to a Declaration of Duties Towards Mankind.* (2001). Routledge Classics.

Weil, Simone. *Waiting for God.* (2009). Harper Perennials.

Weil, Simone. *Notebooks.* (2003). Routledge Classics.

Lewis, Rick. *Philippa Foot.* (2003). Philosophy Now. Accessed on April 27, 2014

Thompson, J. *The Trolley Problem.* (1985). The Yale Law Journal. Accessed on April 27, 2014

O'Grady, Jane. *Philippa Foot Obituary.* (2010). The Guardian. Accessed on April 27, 2014

O'Grady, Jane. *Elizabeth Anscombe.* (2001). The Guardian. Accessed on May 05, 2014

Driver, Julia. *Gertrude Elizabeth Margaret Anscombe.* (2009). Stanford University. Accessed on May 05, 2014

The Telegraph. *Professor G.E.M. Anscombe.* (2001). Accessed on May 05, 2014

Conference on G.E.M. Anscombe, Set for March. *Neumann University.* (2014). Accessed on May 05, 2014

Richter, Duncan. *G.E.M. Anscombe* . Internet Encyclopedia of Philosophy. Accessed on May 05, 2014

Murdoch, Iris. *Metaphysics as a Guide to Morals.* (1993). Penguin.

Williams, Hywel. *Murdoch, an Unlikely Liberal Icon.* (2002). The Guardian. Accessed on May 15, 2014

Ousby, Ian, et al. *Literature in English.* (1993). Cambridge University Press.

Carrington, John. *Our Greatest Writers.* (2003). Howtobooks

Rich, Adrienne. *Of Woman Born.* (1979). Virago.

Arnold, Roxane & Chandler, Olive. *Feminine Singular.* (1975). Femina Books Ltd.

Russell, Bertrand. *History of Western Philosophy.* (1946). George Allen & Unwin, Ltd.

Warnock, Mary. *Making Babies.* (2002). Oxford University Press.

Smith, Wesley J. *The Time Has Come to Outlaw Human Cloning.* (2013). Accessed August 23 2013.

Dawn, R. Owner of John Lennon's tooth hopes to clone the late Beatle.. (2013). NBC. Accessed August 25, 2013.

Midgley, Mary, *Death and the Human Animal.* (2012). Philosophy Now.

Gaspar, Christine, *"Can Transhumanism and the Everyman Co-Exist?"* Institute for Ethics and Emerging Technologies. (2013). Accessed September 15, 2013.

Dowell, B. *David Attenborough: I don't ever want to stop work* (2013). RadioTImes. Accessed September 15, 2013.

Anthony, Andrew. *Late Stand for a Thinker with Soul.* (2014). The Observer. Accessed on April 04, 2014.

Midgley, Martin. *Speech Report on the Fight Against Stupidity.* (2012). Philosophy Now. Accessed on April 04, 2014.

Dawkins, Richard. *The God Delusion.* (2007). Black Swan.

Beard, Mary. *Oh Do Shut Up Dear.* BBC4 Television.

Beard, Mary. The Public Voice of Women. (2014). London Review of Books. Accessed on March 20, 2014

Thank you for reading my book *Eighteen Amazing Women Philosophers*. I hope you enjoyed it and found it informative – and that it will lead you to further exploration and the pleasure of discovery.

## About the Author:

Janet Cameron holds a BA (hons) 2.1 in Literature and Philosophy, and an MA in Modern Poetry with the University of Kent, which incorporates the philosophical manifestos of major poets and the work of controversial founding father of deconstruction in philosophy, Jacques Derrida.

Janet is a retired lecturer at the University of Kent, and an award-winning writer. She is also the author of thirteen books, mostly regional history publications, numerous articles on history, philosophy, feminism and human rights, and short literary fiction. She writes a monthly magazine column for Writers Forum.

Printed in Great Britain
by Amazon